GUTS
AND
GRIT

The Compelling and Inspirational Stories of Six Successful Ghanaian Entrepreneurs

Guts and Grit

The Compelling and Inspirational Stories of Six Successful Ghanaian Entrepreneurs

ISBN for this Edition: 978-9988-9024-0-7

Edited: Kofi Akpabli
Cover design (concept and creation) by Alex Banful
Book Layout by Kuzah John
Email: worldbeststudio2014@gmail.com
Tel: +233 241 456 872 | +233 509 293 248

Published by
DAkpabli & Associates
P O Box 7465, Accra North, Accra, Ghana
Tel: +233 264 339 066 | +233 244 704 250 | +233 247 896 375
Email: info@dakpabli.com

ALEX BANFUL

GUTS
AND
GRIT

The Compelling and Inspirational Stories of Six Successful Ghanaian Entrepreneurs

DAkpabli

SUCCESS IS A LADDER THAT CANNOT BE CLIMBED WITH HANDS IN YOUR POCKET

——African Proverb

DEDICATION

This book is first dedicated to the memory of my parents Jacob and Elizabeth Banful through whose sacrifice, toil, foresight, and dedication to raising, nurturing, and giving equal opportunities to all 8 children and several non-biological ones have made me who I am today.

AND TO

Margaret Banful my wife, who has not only been a solid rock behind me inspiring, motivating, and encouraging me to complete this book, but has also been the major wind beneath my wings propelling me to the heights I reached in my career.

TABLE OF CONTENTS

ACKNOWLEDGEMENT

The book Guts and Grit has come to fruition through the efforts and instrumentality of certain persons and institutions to whom I am deeply indebted. First and foremost, the six Ghanaian entrepreneurs who were so generous with their time and personal stories, without which this book project would never have seen the light of day. I am also deeply indebted to my wife Margaret who kept encouraging me anytime I felt like dropping the project.

I am additionally grateful to my children especially to my daughters Abena Nyarko, Adwoa Nyeekua and Akua Akyeamponmaa who played various roles from advising and looking over my contracts to editing, suggesting different phraseology, and sometimes treating me like a student by marking and grading my scripts.

I am most grateful to Professor Robert E. Hinson formerly of the University of Ghana Business School (UGBS) and currently Deputy Vice-Chancellor of the University of Kigali, Rwanda, who readily agreed to write the foreword to this book.

To Maame Afia Saah Bour- Boakye who helped with the transcription of the recorded interviews with our featured entrepreneurs and to Kofi Akpabli of DAkpabli and Associates who helped with the stories as well as handled the process steps of the publishing of this book.

Finally, I am grateful to the almighty God for giving me the strength, fortitude, and forbearance to see this almost decade-and-a-half long project to fruition.

"Thee will I praise with all my heart" -MHB80

FOREWORD

It is indeed my pleasure to write this foreword for Guts and Grit, by my father, mentor, and friend Alex Banful. Guts and Grit is a book that chronicles the gut-wrenching stories of entrepreneurs who have braved significant odds to build viable businesses in a developing economy context. This book is especially relevant because for years Alex himself was in the early 2000s the epitome of entrepreneurial excellence when he led the highly successful Ghana Social Marketing Foundation (GSMF).

In that time, Alex supported the research and presentation of a conference paper entitled Profiling a social marketing leader in Ghana at the 6th International Academy of African Business and Development (IAABD) Conference, which was hosted by the University of Dar-as-Salaam at the Golden Tulip Hotel Dar es Salaam. This paper I co-authored with Alex won a best paper award, and today I am indeed privileged to graduate from co-author to foreword scripter for this most illuminating book.

In choosing to write this book, Alex could not have made a better choice. The choice of entrepreneurship should not be surprising, given that there is at least four decades of scholarship to demonstrate that entrepreneurship, new business venturing, and the development of small and medium enterprises is crucial to Africa's growth. Additionally, a June 2021 African Development Bank White Paper, "Entrepreneurship and Free Trade: Africa's Catalysts for a New Era of Economic Prosperity", states that entrepreneurship must be at the heart of efforts to transform Africa's economic prospects (https://www.afdb.org/en/news-and-events/entrepreneurship-critical-africas-transformation-africandevelopment-bank-44309), The white paper argues further that a number of trends that could bring about more inclusive economic growth are beginning to take hold and that the right interventions could open the door for the continent's young and dynamic entrepreneurs and help build linkages with the large firms that are the key drivers of supply chains to create jobs and revenues to help scale-up businesses.

It is safe to argue that for entrepreneurship to really make an impact on Africa's economic fortunes, there is a dire need for practical texts that chronicle the pains, joys, and triumphs of African businesspersons who are fearless enough to embark on the new venture creation process and excel at it. Guts and Grit will soon become a leading cross-over entrepreneurship textbook that will be useful for executive training, undergraduate and postgraduate training programmes in Africa and other emerging economy contexts. In Alex's own words, this book captures "the heart-rending yet inspiring stories of six Ghanaian entrepreneurs who have defied all the odds" to succeed. All said this book details a step-by-step exposition of entrepreneurial management principles and how they apply to an emerging economy context.

Alex has identified challenges often associated with entrepreneurial management in the African environment, suggested a framework for analysing key issues, and created strategic entrepreneurial action plans that will help new business ventures to emerge as winners in the face of market obstacles. Students and practitioners committed to developing winning entrepreneurial strategies will find in this book both theoretical and practical views of entrepreneurial management with case studies, that are relevant to the challenges and solutions in the modern African market.

In Chapter One of the book, Alex sets the scene for the book falling on the thesis that the promotion of entrepreneurship in Africa is crucial as it creates jobs, provides decent livelihoods, and contributes to GDP. He identifies some critical characteristics of an entrepreneurial mindset and introduces us to the six entrepreneurs who constitute the central characters in this book.

The ensuing chapters of the book focus on how the featured entrepreneurs took apprenticeships seriously and how these apprenticeships gave them hands-on experience and tremendous training to prepare them for the future. In an Africa where the spirit of apprenticeship seems to be disappearing in the light of get-rich-quick mentalities, these stories provide warnings on business discretion and not revealing too much to value chain partners in developing a business idea.

The featured stories teach the reader that being able to start a business with very little money is eloquent testimony to the fact that for entrepreneurial success, a perfect start does not always guarantee future success. Rather, start small, no matter how imperfect and insignificant it could be; with fortitude and perseverance, you could end up building a global brand of immense international repute.

The stories of all the entrepreneurs covered in the book taken together ultimately teach us two major things: First, risk-taking is still an important element of most successful entrepreneurs.

Finally, most of the entrepreneurs displayed stubbornness in their childhood and this is a trait they fell on when they encountered rough patches on their entrepreneurial journey. Alex's admonition as a result, is that it is not all that negative for a growing child to display a strongly determined will. Alex believes that in creating the next generation of entrepreneurs in Ghana/Africa, African parents should look to nurture and properly channel strong-willed and determined tendencies in their children as this trait comes in handywhen the tough times in the development of their future businesses come along.

Guts and Grit is a sure winner and a must-read for business students and practitioners on the African continent and beyond. Entrepreneurs looking for ways to motivate their employees, identify strategies to increase market share, and achieve organisational goals will find value in this book. Undergraduate and Graduate students will find it to be an excellent springboard to a great business life.

I am pleased to highly recommend this book for two reasons. First, while Alex has organised this book into systematic case studies, it is practical, easy to read, and easy to understand. The second reason to be interested in this book is that it is not only current on academic literature, but it also has a world of knowledge about the Ghanaian market.

Alex Banful has developed a book that will be useful for practitioners, professors, and students of entrepreneurship in Africa and beyond.

Robert E. Hinson, Ph.D., DPhil
Deputy Vice-Chancellor
University of Kigali, Rwanda

PROLOGUE

"Someone is sitting in the shade today because someone planted a tree a long-time ago"

Warren Buffet

Entrepreneurship and the development of private enterprises have been the bedrock of the developed world with governments providing the catalytic environment for their growth. Entrepreneurship matters and developing countries have a lot to learn. In Ghana, we have specific problems both systems derived and environmentally compounded, that are barriers to entrepreneurship.

I know from personal experience how tough these can be, both from running my own business and from mentoring many young people who shudder in the face of these odds. This book is being written to inspire and provide a roadmap to young people, using homegrown stories of success. The message is this: "it can be done", and my hope is that officialdom and society, in general, will dismantle the legacies that perpetuate the hostile environment and create an environment that catalyses business growth.

These stories of successful people are akin to both planting and nurturing dreams and aspirations of would-be entrepreneurs whose resilience and tenacity are so tested that many give up. These stories told will hopefully become the seed for the success of future enterprises.

Whilst researching for this book, I was struck by the strong reticence amongst the most successful businesspersons to share their stories. I discovered that the "fear of being noticed" at the forefront and targeted is a major reason for their reticence. There is a perception that private businesses use inappropriate methods to succeed, and it is apparent that the tax and other regulatory authorities seem to be forever looking to prove the truth of this perception.

Hence, a mere spotlight on any business immediately triggers crippling tax audits and other inquisitive prying from other regulatory authorities.

I am not suggesting that businesses should be allowed to cheat to succeed. However, the hostility exhibited by some of the regulatory authorities pushes businesses to not only keep a low profile but reduces the desire to achieve mega sizes and forays into the international arena. High interest rates and a hostile banking environment have also served to deny the resources most companies would need to move to scale.

In the words of one of the entrepreneurs who was kind enough to tell their stories when asked about banking support: "When you start or run a business your financing is between you, yourself, and your God."

The reason for this book is to start the process of the dismantling of the obstacles, real and imagined, and be able to get additional entrepreneurs to be more willing to tell their stories to serve as a source of inspiration and a springboard to the young people who would be willing to take up the mantle. It also serves to shine a light on the hostile environment with the hope that officialdom will begin to start dismantling some of the obstacles to achieving business success.

The teeming numbers of unemployed young persons can only be solved with the growth of business industries, not government jobs. Therefore, the requisite ingredients of a friendly catalysing environment must be gingered and generated.

There is, however, another side to the unfriendly environment, and this is even stronger than the structural institutional barriers and attitude. The attitude of the society at large, either discouraging people from embarking on their own ventures or going to work for a new entrepreneur, has become a major factor in this regard.

One of our colonial relics is the issue of linking certain types and levels of education to certain types of jobs. Thus, when one has had tertiary education, it is expected that one will pick up a government job or a prestigious private sector position. Therefore, when one suggests starting something on their own the general impression is that this is a failure who lacks the confidence to fight for a position in a reputable company. The social pressure alone is enough to dissuade a budding entrepreneur from seeing the larger environment and opportunities, not to talk about almost zero financial avenues available to motivate them to take the plunge.

This book, therefore, aims to start the process of bridging this gap by highlighting the success stories of some of our current entrepreneurs despite all the obstacles they have faced, and that even as tough as it is to get things moving, it is doable. It is also to serve as a revelation to our public officials and the society at large towards a behavioural change in how private enterprises are seen, regarded, and treated. The derogation that the term "one-man business" connotes is enough to discourage many a person from either embarking on the journey of creating an enterprise or working for one.

What is needed is a change in attitude from the society, to encourage, rather than to discourage budding entrepreneurs as well as change the perception that well-educated persons need to be employed by someone rather than being self-employed. Currently, the government jobs and the seemingly attractive private sector positions are just a shade short of 1.5 million people. Therefore, if we are not to glorify groupings like the Unemployed Graduates Associations and their ilk, a joint effort of both officialdom and the society will aid in the provision of the right tools and environment for the growth of the job market and by extension the economy and sustainability of businesses.

The stories highlighted in the book indicate some of the gut-wrenching issues these entrepreneurs have had to deal with and the sheer grit that has been needed to stay afloat. These are persons who refused to back down and have surmounted obstacles to achieve the success stories we are now gladly happy to tell.The change in both the structural and environmental factors militating against entrepreneurship growth must change and it starts from now.

Alex Banful
Accra.

CHAPTER 1

INTRODUCTION

"Strength does not come from physical capacity. It comes from an indomitable will."

Mahatma Gandhi

The world has only one constant variable and that is change. All progressive societies require a change to continue to stay relevant and to grow. Entrepreneurs and leaders lead and manage change in the process of transforming their societies and economies.Transformational leaders according to (Pierce and Newstrom-2000) move and change things in a big way not by offering tokens of inducement but through the inspiration of others.They are individuals who through personal values, vision, passion and a commitment to a mission energise and move others. From the perspective of Podsakoff, Mackenzie et al, (1990),Transformational leadership is multi-dimensional in nature and lists six key behaviours associated with transformational leadership. These are (1) identifying and articulating a vision, (2) providing an appropriate model, (3) fostering the acceptance of group goals, (4) high-performance expectations, (5) providing individualised support, and (6) Intellectual stimulation.

Entrepreneurship refers to the process of creating a new enterprise and bearing any of its risks, with the view of making a profit. Therefore, the person who creates a new enterprise and embraces every challenge for its development and operation is known as an entrepreneur.

Timmons's (1990) Model of Entrepreneurship states that entrepreneurship is opportunity-driven, or that the market shapes the opportunity.

A good idea is not necessarily a good business opportunity, and the underlying market demand determines the potential of the idea. An idea becomes viable only when it remains anchored in products or services that create or add value to customers, and remains attractive, durable, and timely. The model considers opportunities, teams, and resources as the three critical factors available to an entrepreneur and holds that success depends on the ability of the entrepreneur to balance these critical factors. The entrepreneur risks his or her career, personal cash flow, and net worth. The Timmons model of the entrepreneurial process has three key elements: opportunity, team and resources.

These must fit together and should be properly aligned in conjunction with each other in order to make the business plan successful (Timmons, 1990). Contrary to this, (Shane, 2003) in his model argues that; entrepreneurial opportunities arise from the individual as well as environmental factors, which lead to discovering and exploiting opportunities and executing the whole business plan in a successful manner.

Goosen and Stevenson (2013) describe the phenomenon characterised as entrepreneurial leadership which is a term that will be used repeatedly in this book. They indicate that "without leadership, great ideas never become embodied. But at the same time, people that are gifted in coordinating work and workers – managers also may not be entrepreneurs as they do not bring to their leadership; innovation, seizing opportunities and creating."

The writer of this book prefers the use of the term "entrepreneurial leadership", not exactly from the perspective of Goosen and Stevenson. It is the belief of the author that both entrepreneurship and leadership retain interchangeable roles, skills, and characteristics. Both concepts speak to a vision, a translation of the vision into actuality, and the mobilisation of people behind the vision to achieve the desired results. Leaders are entrepreneurial and entrepreneurs are leaders. It is in this context that the combined term entrepreneurial leadership will be used in this book.

The Ghanaian entrepreneurial and transformational leadership skills have been at play from time immemorial. This resulted in the rise of a small group of merchants who succeeded mostly in the retail trade or as timber merchants. This group, all of them self-made entrepreneurs, endured the harsh conditions of an unfriendly economic environment and succeeded, despite having to navigate restrictions put in place by successive colonial governments; after independence, they received no sympathy amidst a state-led industrialisation drive that was hostile to the private sector, and that, unfairly, associated entrepreneurship with labor exploitation.

With the passage of the Ghanaian Business Promotion Act in 1970, a new wind of change started blowing, working to place Ghanaians in charge of their nation's industry and economy. Under the act, all foreign companies were to divest of a minimum of 55% of their shares to Ghanaians. This act clearly sought to promote the entrepreneurial instinct of the Ghanaian. Fifty years after this act, and after many subsequent policies meant to stimulate homegrown entrepreneurship and industry, there are only a few successful Ghanaian innovators whose enterprises have attained the size these legislative acts were meant to encourage.

In 2001, there was a paradigm shift, a newly elected government came into office and declared a vision of a private sector-led growth economy and for the first time set up a ministerial unit to pursue this vision. Without a doubt, the private sector that has been touted as the engine of growth is a real engine to produce the trajectory for growth. But engines differ in size and power, from twin-stroke motorbike engines to powerful turbine-based aircraft engines. The big question, therefore, has been what type and how powerful an engine will have the capacity to produce this massive change from a state-led economy to a private sector-engineered one. The fact is that the public sector through facilitative policies becomes the vehicle for this engine to function. The size and capacity of the facilitation determine the power that the engine of growth can exert.

The purpose of this book is to chronicle the heart-rending, yet inspiring stories of six (6) Ghanaian entrepreneurs who have defied all the odds, fought against the system survived and failed and survived again to keep this dream of moving over to a private sector-engineered economy. Persons who put their personal comfort at risk, forgoing the security their peers sought in government or multinational jobs, these entrepreneurs risked all they had to create viable businesses. In a notoriously hostile business environment, their companies have stood the test of time by surviving for 10 or more years.

These stories are meant first and foremost to inspire younger readers to consider charting their own entrepreneurial paths; but, more importantly, this study will draw parallels and find common threads between and amongst the stories of these entrepreneurs. In so doing, this book will shine a light on what keeps these pioneers going despite all the odds and obstacles they have faced in their business journeys.

This study will discuss the processes, developments, and approaches that our featured entrepreneurs have used to achieve their successes. Itwill also look at their entrepreneurial and leadership skills and lessons that can be deduced from how they have carried on despite the challenges.

Over the course of this book, we will explore some of the entrepreneurship characteristics that Goossen and Stevens (2013) in their book Entrepreneurial Leadership have discussed as the makeup of the essence of entrepreneurship. The six business leaders covered in this book have displayed a dogged ability to keep going despite setbacks. This is the hallmark of all successful entrepreneurs and leaders. To get talented individuals to sign on when the enterprise is young requires leadership. To mold these individuals into a team also require leadership skills.

These are some of the key characteristics of entrepreneurial leaders, especially within the Ghanaian context who decide to endure the rewards and heartbreaks of taking on the thankless never-ending mission of growing a business.

Innovation:

This is believed to be the most essential tenet of entrepreneurship. It is the ability to do something new, unique, and different and to satisfy a need in the marketplace. Innovation does not only mean new products or services but new and better ways of delivering an old product or service; for example, using digital technology to deliver convenience. An innovator role, therefore, is the pursuit of a difference, and the market subsequently rewards this effort.

Seizing Opportunities:

Entrepreneurs, recognize, seize and pursue opportunities to innovate. They see change as normal, as healthy, and as an opportunity, whether the change is in the market, in technology, in delivery modes or in the culture. Successful businesspeople screen incoming information in a different way. Since they constantly seek new growth opportunities, an entrepreneur acts on the possibility that an identified opportunity is worth pursuing. Entrepreneurs immerse fully in the newly identified opportunity and therefore are participants, not spectators

Strong Internal Motivation

The "Fire Inside". The motivation that drives our behavior comes from two sources: internal (intrinsic) and external (extrinsic). Intrinsic factors include constructs like needs, desires, motives, and willpower. Extrinsic factors include any type of motivational influence from the environment such as rewards and punishments.

For entrepreneurs, the most important motivational factor is the intrinsic one. Entrepreneurs keep going even though everyone tells them that they are wasting their time. When the intrinsic drive goes away, so does any chance of success. In short, entrepreneurs must have a clear sense of fulfillment and satisfaction. Money is never the primary motivation for a successful entrepreneur. Entrepreneurs sometimes pursue a passion despite limited financial rewards but for its altruistic values.

Courage

Entrepreneurs are mostly referred to as risks takers. Another way is to say that one must have guts. It requires a great deal of courage to build a company from the ground up.

Someone once explained that large organisations function like "wombs" protecting employees from a harsh and unforgiving environment. It takes a great deal of courage to leave a corporate or government womb and to strike out by oneself into the cold, cruel world of business. When one first starts a business, one is alone, and the entrepreneur must often make decisions in highly uncertain environments where time as well as emotional and monetary pressures are immense.The courage to undertake the risk assessments and still plod on is an important characteristic. No matter how careful an entrepreneur might be there will always be some level of risk, and this cannot be wished away.

Optimism

The underlying foundation of successful entrepreneurs is a boundless fount of optimism that never seems to end. When faced with a problem, they view it as a challenge. When faced with a setback, they view it as a new direction. This optimism contrasts sharply with most people who project a more pessimistic, defeatist view. It's this belief in the positive that serves as a foundation for dealing with the many setbacks one will inevitably encounter in the world of business.

Developing an entrepreneurial mindset:

A critical characteristic is an entrepreneurial mindset. Sometimes, it is referred to as traits. These include willingness and determination, opportunity obsession, tolerance of risk, ambiguity and uncertainty, creativity, self-reliance, and a motivation to succeed, no matter the obstacles. Even though a lot of these traits are inherited, they can also be mastered through training and exposure.

Suffice it to say, entrepreneurs passionately seek and pursue new opportunities. They focus on innovation and execution harnessing the skills and energies of all within their domain. The challenges that most Ghanaian entrepreneurs have faced and continue to face make it near impossible for the weak and faint-hearted to dream of entering the arena. A difficult business terrain, unsympathetic bank officials, unfriendly regulatory officials, and an unending list of challenges have been the bane of many an entrepreneur who has tried to get a business going and growing in Ghana.

This has led to small and micro enterprises that are one-person enterprises or at best, employ a handful of people. From time immemorial an indomitable entrepreneurial spirit and skill have dominated the landscape of Ghana. Statistics indicate that about 80% of the population is in some form of personal enterprise spanning the whole scope of the business ecosystem.

However, most of these have remained as small and subsistence enterprises with very few emerging as large enough enterprises to create employment and a reasonable income for the owners. The main reason for this situation is a harsh, difficult, distrustful, and unhelpful climate perpetrated by state regulators, poor financial and unhelpful cultural environment. This situation makes most would-be entrepreneurs resign to just doing enough for themselves and their small family circle's subsistence.

However, it is not for the want of skill or acumen but is a result of the environment or lack thereof for fostering entrepreneurial growth. Despite this harsh terrain and climate, some Ghanaians have braved the odds to establish viable businesses and seen them through the growth cycles.

A PARADE OF PORTRAITS

CELEBRATING GHANAIAN ENTREPRENEURIAL LEADERS

Anthony (Tony) Oteng–Gyasi

Leticia Osafo-Addo

Gwyneth Gyimah Addo

Kwasi Appiagyei

Kofi Anku

Theresa Oppong Beeko

Anthony (Tony) Oteng–Gyasi: Founder and Chairman, Tropical Cable and Conductor Manufacturing Company

Tony Oteng-Gyasi is a successful businessman who made it through hard work from selling pallets to establishing his own electrical conductor and cables producing company. His most resonating character is his resilience and belief in being the first to start something where no one dared to venture. From failed partnered ventures to a booming wooden crate business, Tony was the carpenter who never used a hammer but was the best at his wood business and a great marketing executive. Currently, his company, Tropical Cable and Conductors, is amongst the best cable companies in the country and in the sub-region. He likes to tread where no souls have trod, and risk seems to be in his DNA. In his own words, "Even if I lost everything, I would gladly take a risk at business all over again."

Leticia Osafo-Addo: Founder and CEO, Samba Foods

Leticia Osafo-Addo trained as an Intensive Care Nurse but saw an opportunity to venture into pepper farming as a side business that eventually became the dominant business. This led her to study and obtain an MBA in Management Technology and Innovation. It started with her first and best investment in a pepper seed. She is now the CEO of Samba Foods, a food processing company wholly Ghanaian owned. Her pepper seed has made it to all parts of the world and to every home in Ghana.

Samba Foods provides essential materials for food to big players in the industry in Ghana. Leticia Osafo-Addo knows the magic of small. Start small and aim for the top in a grand style. She has through her ups and downs survived and beaten the odds to be recognised for her hard work. She believes in building one's dream, giving new twists to the plot mapped out so the end results become better than the original dream. She has a strong belief in her Christian faith anchored with ethical principles and garnished with ingenuity. Her "never say never" spirit has seen her through the growth from that pepper seed to a big industrial organisation.

Gwyneth Gyimah Addo: Founder and CEO, Hair Senta

Gwen's passion and attitude for herwork have been pivotal to her success as an entrepreneur. She is the CEO of Hair Senta, Ghana's premier hair shop that provides that exceptional avenue for a variety of hair. At Hair Senta, one is spoilt for choice and that is exactly what Gwen set out to achieve. A Philosophy major and an MBA graduate, Gwen lives her mantra "we compete on exceptional customer experience" daily. The entrepreneurial journey for Gwen has been tough but her resilience and commitment has seen her reach her current heights. She started her hair selling business from her car boot; left a cushy stable job at Standard Chartered Bank to pursue the unknown, her entrepreneurial dream. Currently, her business spans Ghana, Togo, Nigeria, Europe, and North America.

Kwasi Appiagyei: Founder and CEO, Adat Water and Allied Companies

Kwasi Appiagyei is the CEO of Adat Industries, a firm that was practically built from the scraps of a dead manufacturing firm. His frenetic attack towards challenges is one of his adored attributes. He believed in his dreams to never compromise after his first failure. No matter the dead ends he came to on his way up the ladder, he still stuck to his motto of consistency. In all, he believes he is his own source of success. He is into the production of purified drinking water and provides supplies to ensure consistent water quality for various manufacturing industries that use water as a major input for their products. Kwasi sees opportunities rather than difficulties when solving problems.

Kofi Anku: Executive Director, Volta (Ghana) Investments Co. Ltd and Partner, Ayi Mensah Park

Kofi Anku is an American-born Ghanaian. He is a partner of the heart-warming picturesque Ayi Mensah Park and Estates. He had the vision to provide world-class construction for people with dreams of owning no-worries houses in a luxurious environment. Kofi is a finely chiseled businessman who straddles the best in terms of culture and finesse by virtue of both the US and Ghanaian environments that he had the privilege of being brought up in. He describes himself as a strong believer of the pan-African dream, one he swam his way towards as his new freedom, his new armour for finer things formed here in Ghana. Kofi's strong grounding in ethical business practices has led him through the ups and downs of developing enterprises. His dream and imagination is the beautifully laid-out Ayi-Mensah Park at the foot of the Aburi hills.

Theresa Oppong Beeko: Founder and CEO of Manet Housing Estates

The woman who only sees beauty in hewn bricks fused with wood and some paint. Theresa is a trained Sociologist with an MBA and the founder and owner of Manet Real Estate company with state-of-the-art housing estates of uniquely made homes. Her passion had always been seeing bits and pieces of wood and finely mixed concrete all coming together to create elegant houses. Endurance and perseverance are her daily dose of motivation. She took an initiative with a strong will and not only survived but excelled in what was seen then as a man's world. For someone whose private passion is reading romantic novels, it is an appealing sight to see her other passion of helmets, jeans, and architectural drawings.

Conclusion

The foregoing is a summary of profiles of our featured entrepreneurs who have displayed an indomitable will to succeed in the face of severe challenges and a hostile business environment. Theirs is not a case of not having options to take a cushy job but with risk and success as part of their DNA, there is little wonder they chose the paths they trod armed with visions, enthusiasm, a never-say-never spirit, and ethical grounding to achieve their dreams despite obstacles. These have shown entrepreneurial leadership and time has proved their choices right.

The next few chapters will profile each person's story as a case study written with a biographical approach but told in both a narrative and conversational style. We explore their ups and downs and the driving forces that have kept their faith on the path to succeed and achieve the heights they have reached providing jobs and livelihoods to teeming numbers of Ghanaians.

These are Ghanaians whose achievements are worthy of celebration as an example to the up-and-coming generation to continue with the efforts despite the still unfriendly terrain.

They have really shown not only the ***Guts*** to enter the hostile business terrain but also the ***Grit*** to hold on and succeed.

CASE STUDY ONE

ANTHONY (TONY) OTENG GYASI

CHAPTER 2

THE OBSTINACY OF OPTIMISM

TONY OTENG-GYASI

"Take a chance! All life is a chance. The man who goes farthest is the one willing to do and dare."

Dale Carnegie

Even from his school days, Tony Oteng-Gyasi was curious and a voracious reader. If any moment would confirm that, it would be the day he found himself totally engrossed in the soiled sheet of paper that had been used to wrap his roadside kelewele, which eventually became his Northern Star and pointed him in the direction of his company, Tropical Cable and Conductors. He could not help but laugh at himself. He was too far gone.

His is a story of dogged tenacity, an unbending desire to get what he wanted, but at the same time not always knowing what exactly that was. And yet, in his lifelong craving to satisfy his curiosity, he would stumble upon the very things that would make him stand out.

Tony's life began on 15th February 1955 in Krofrom, Kumasi. Thereafter, the family moved to Ashanti New Town, also in Kumasi. His arrival after three girls on the trot was celebrated, but before long, the family dynamic changed. In those days, it was not uncommon for young Ashanti men to chance a trip down south to make a fortune in Accra, the capital. The family would thus come visiting at Christmas and during school holidays, because Tony's three sisters were in school in Kumasi. After one trip when Tony was perhaps four years old, he threw a mighty tantrum at the Accra train station, refusing to go back to Kumasi. The sight of the poor boy in a flood of tears broke the family's heart and they left him behind with his father. After all, he was not in school yet.

As a young man in newly independent Ghana, Tony's father was starting a business from the ground up as a sand and stone contractor. Tony would go with him to win sand at the beach at Chorkor every now and then, but his father did not know what to do with his young son, and promptly enrolled him in Snaps Preparatory School in Asylum Down at the age of five. Though his parents would not be counted among the educated elite – his father was a Middle School Level Certificate holder and his mother sold plantains in the Kumasi market – they were determined to give their children access to better opportunities through education than they had.

He remembers an American lady who taught them religion once or twice a week through Bible stories that Tony enjoyed. In contrast, he also remembered being whipped in class for not paying attention during maths class.

During the early 1960s, schoolchildren were gathered on the grounds of the Flagstaff House during the president's birthday celebrations in late September to interact with him. They would sit in little groups on the green lawn while Dr Kwame Nkrumah, the republic's president, talked to the various groups for about an hour. Unknown to him, while Tony spoke to the president, the exchange was caught on film. Those were the days that Information Services vans would go around different communities, allowing citizens to gather around them to watch the news. Tony's brief interaction with President Nkrumah made it to the final cut, and in Ashanti New Town, where his mother lived, everyone saw him. That was his claim to fame in the community, far away in Kumasi from his home.

Before long, the rest of the family was reunited permanently, this time in Adabraka, Accra. His father had found some success in business and could afford basic comforts for the family in a smaller housing unit within a big house. For example, they were one of a few households that had a refrigerator. In what was perhaps a nod towards future entrepreneurial activity, Tony would barter ice-cold water for a piece of fried fish with a kenkey seller in the area, though this was an arrangement initiated by the seller.

Having started school at a younger age than his classmates, Tony found that his interests always seemed at odds with the rest of the class. Perhaps it also had to do with his own interests lying elsewhere. In maths class, his mind would wander to a story from an earlier class. He preferred memorising his lines for his part in "Merchant of Venice", a Shakespeare play the school was going to perform. He was more about what he wanted to do than what he had to do. At the same time, he did just enough to pass all his classes and never failed, a mark that he maintained throughout his entire education journey.

At the age of 10, Tony wrote his Common Entrance Examinations to enter the next phase of his education. He got admitted to Swedru Secondary School (SWESCO). Apart from a short stint in boarding school at Snaps before his mother and sisters came to Accra, this was the first time he had to spend a considerable amount of time away from home.

He was homesick from the very beginning, and still being younger than his classmates, he considered that another level of difficulty. At the weekends, his sister would come for his dirty laundry and take it back to Accra to be washed. By the end of the second term, though, he was more comfortable doing his own laundry. The teasing from mates and seniors most likely sped up this decision.

SWESCO played a big part in shaping Tony's identity. Having arrived in Accra during his formative years, Tony spoke better Ga than he did Twi, and so he opted for Ga lessons when he had a choice to make for vernacular as a subject. He even went as far as faking a Ga name for himself – using the name of one of his playmates in Adabraka – so as not to raise too many questions. It was only after he came home on vacation and his father impressed on him to use the opportunity to learn proper Twi that he made the switch to the Twi class.

One day, he got summoned to the headmaster's office. This was odd. The headmaster told Tony that he did not think he would survive boarding school without some extra attention. To make his experience a little less stressful, the headmaster gave him an open invitation to his house to have a meal of fufu on Saturdays. Unfortunately, Tony was not a fan of fufu, having grown up on Ga tastes. He never took up the offer.

Maybe the headmaster spotted him because of how young he was. Maybe it was because he came from a preparatory school, and so was considered softer than most. Or maybe he stood out for his notable ease with the English language. "My seniors would call me just to ask me questions and hear me rattling away," he remembered.

It was during his SWESCO years that Tony realised how much he loved to read. He discovered the Edgar Wallace series of novels, reading in bed with a torchlight after lights out. Even in Form One, he was reading "Tell Freedom: Memories of Africa" by South African writer Peter Abrahams. This was the novel the seniors had to study for their O-Levels, and here was this precocious young boy breezing through it for fun. The seniors would call him, and they would talk about the book for their own revision. He was answering context questions even before he knew what that was. He knew who said what in the book. It came so naturally to him. He even joined the Debating Society, making a name for himself as "that Form One boy who can talk".

As he entered his teenage years, life in secondary school was normal: a fight here and there, and strict adherence to times and schedules. He was more likely to get in trouble for not being able to wake up early after spending much of the night reading.

Even before Tony knew that he wanted to be an entrepreneur, traits would pop up in him every now and then. By Form Four, he was organising trips back home to Accra for students. It was not an original idea. Students were doing it before he got to SWESCO, and others had their organised trips. A senior of his got him involved because he possessed a gift in convincing people to join their bus when he went round with his pen and paper to get commitments.

It was around that same time that his father began to rope him into the family business. His first real training in sales started during vacations from Form Three. His father was now a cement distributor. Having established himself in Accra and Kumasi, he gradually opened depots around other parts of the country. Takoradi around Market Circle was where young Tony got his feet wet.

During his long vacation that year, he went to visit his father. There was a place called the Axim Station, where all the vehicles coming from the Axim and Nzema areas came to, about 40 metres from Market Circle. Tony's father got another shop in the Axim Station itself, meaning that prospective buyers were saved the walk from the Market Circle, albeit short, to buy their cement.

Though the depot was new, they were making sales of between 1,000 and 2,000 bags a day in that Axim Station shop. Because it was new, nobody had been recruited yet, meaning that Tony ran the shop all by himself, calculating total cost, collecting the money, and issuing receipts. At noon, he would take all his collections to the main shop at Market Circle, from where it would be taken to the Barclays Bank there. Trust meant increased responsibility, and over the course of the vacation, Tony was given his own pay-in book.

He took his apprenticeship seriously. It was a hands-on experience and tremendous training for one so young. He learned how to use the reckoner. (Before the era of calculators, this was a handbook of tables to facilitate computation).

He grew accustomed to basic banking and handling cash on-site, from counting and dividing into denominations to giving change to buyers. While it was serious business, it was also fun. Friends who were based in Takoradi came to the shop when they could to offer help.

As business flourished over time, Tony also grew in confidence: "Eventually, I had a shop assistant and a watchman. Those were my two employees, as it were, who were under my command. So, I told the watchman and the shop assistant to carry 20 bags to this vehicle, 30 bags to this truck, and they would sit with me until I closed the shop at 6:00 pm or 6:30 pm." After depositing the money at the main store, they would go off to Princess Cinema to watch a movie.

In 1969, when Tony was in Form Four, the Dr. Kofi Abrefa Busia-led government declared an Open General Licence in the budget. The implications of this were clear among the traders of Takoradi Market Circle. It meant that anybody could import anything into the country to sell. Tony's father took advantage of this as well and imported tonnes of sugar. The problem, though, was that many others also imported sugar, leading to a glut and many of the traders losing their wares to spoilage. The lesson here was that everybody can recognise an opportunity, but what really counts is how this opportunity is handled.

After passing his O-Levels, it was now time to go to Sixth Form. He selected Sekondi College for two reasons. The first was that it was one of the few institutions that offered his preferred combination of Economics, Geography, and English. Secondly, he had managed to influence a lot of his mates from SWESCO with his wild tales of Takoradi, so about five of them made plans to experience the vibrant twin cities of Sekondi-Takoradi for themselves. How could he distance himself from the action?

Sekondi College was a totally different experience from SWESCO. The freedom they had as students was mind-blowing. They could not believe it. Where SWESCO was run by timetables and threats of punishment, the laxity in Sekondi College was shocking. Students could spend whole days in town, and nobody seemed to notice.

The silver lining was that Tony was forced to learn time management. If the school would not run on a schedule, he would have to do it for himself. With students coming from different schools – Prempeh College, Achimota School, Mfantsipim School, Oda Secondary School, Accra High School, and Accra Academy among others – he picked up their study methods. He was able to learn to do the same thing in different ways.

Tony imbibed the power of focus. He learned to prioritise. He internalised delayed gratification. Reading was still a huge part of his life, but he understood that there were other things he needed to complete before he could binge on five or six novels that he had stockpiled for himself. Gone were the days of his youth where he would be found leisurely reading a novel the day before an exam.

They had a young lady who had graduated from the University of Ghana teaching them Geography. She told them about the First University Exams (FUE) and about life in Legon and more. Tony was sold. This was what he wanted as well, and so he was ready to make the sacrifices needed to get there. Looking back, the biggest lesson from his two years at Sekondi College was that you can have too much of a good thing to your ultimate detriment.

To stay engaged in school life, he joined the Debating Society in Sekondi College as well but made time for his studies. He was not a prefect, though he was a school executive for the Ghana United Nations Students Association (GUNSA). All these continued to build his confidence as a leader.

By his own admission, he did not study hard enough for his O-Levels. He was a different man when A-Levels came around and went into the examinations full of confidence. Unfortunately, for some of his mates, they were unable to handle the independence and fell to the allure of life outside the school walls when they should have been in school. There were many who failed, which meant that Sekondi College did not have a good success rate for university admission.

While he was succeeding in the classroom, business was growing. His father had employed full-time staff for all his shops, so he only played a supervisory role during vacations and after his A-Levels. He would keep an eye on things since his father travelled a lot.

By the time he was entering the University of Ghana, Tony was thinking about the future more. What career path would he want to pursue? In his first year, he studied Economics, Geography, and Sociology, reckoning that there was not much he could do with a degree in English. Besides, his insatiable urge to read could always be satisfied through casual reading. He discovered that he liked Sociology as well. However, he reasoned that Economics gave him the best chance at a bright future in trading, commerce, or business, and so he pursued that. It also helped that he had fallen in love with Economics.

Since he had not done any form of mathematics since his O-Levels, and he would need a maths background to succeed, Tony got his roommate, an Agriculture major, to teach him Add Maths. While most of his time was devoted to schoolwork, though, he got involved in the campaign for a friend as Students' Representative Council (SRC) Secretary. This activity forced Tony to stretch himself again, this time having to brainstorm ideas for election posters. Unconsciously, he was training himself in branding and marketing.

After three years in Legon, it was time to go out into the world. Here, his choice of major helped him a great deal, opening a way for him to be posted to the Bank of Ghana for his national service. As far as Tony could see, this was the hand of providence at work, as his batch, the class of 1975, was among the first to be posted to the central bank after the Bank of Ghana wrote to the Department of Economics, asking them to recommend high-potential recent graduates. This resulted in two of them being picked.

He knew his employment was a one-year national service, so while he was there, a myriad of thoughts swirled through Tony's mind as to what was next for him. Banking? Finance? Accountancy? Surveying the landscape, however, he decided to go the marketing route, seeing as it was a new area in Ghana in the 1970s.

"While doing my national service, I registered with the Chartered Institute of Marketing (CIM) UK and Rapid Results Correspondence Course studying marketing," Tony recalled. "So, by the end of the year, I had completed both Certificate One and Certificate Two. I got some exemptions because of my Economics degree."

His all-around diligence paid off. Dr Jackson, his boss, asked him to stay on for another year with the promise of helping him pursue a post-graduate degree. Being in the Research Department was opportune. This is the powerhouse of the bank where monetary policy is concerned. And since Dr Jackson had published a well-received paper in the bank's bulletin with Tony's research assistance, the boss knew this was a prospect to hold on to.

As fate would have it, though, the Bank of Ghana was not the only hunter in the chase for Tony's talents. He had applied to United Africa Company (UAC), which years later merged with Lever Brothers to form Unilever. He also applied and was interviewed at British American Tobacco (BAT) and British Petroleum (BP). While BAT and UAC invited Tony for a second interview, BP presented a firm offer. By this time, his two options were staying at the Bank of Ghana or going to BP.

In the end, the higher salary offered by BP swung the pendulum in their favour. Besides, BP's offer was more inclined to a marketing role, while it was finance in the central bank, which Tony was trying to distance himself from by now.

That is how at the age of 21, Tony Oteng-Gyasi started his career at BP as a management trainee in the Marketing Department, the youngest ever at the time to have joined the company.

He was sent to the Consumer Sales Department after his induction and six-month probation. Lessons he learned there stuck with him throughout his life. One of his first assignments was in divestiture. It was 1977, and BP had a lot of locked-up profit in Ghana. The military leader of Ghana, Gen Ignatius Kutu Acheampong, and his government had just come out with a policy saying that if BP and other multinational companies put their profits into another investment, then whatever profit came out of that investment could be transferred in its entirety without question. The nation was suffering under the weight of severe foreign exchange problems at the time, which made this a prudent decision. BP thus proceeded to look at various investment possibilities in Ghana, and this job fell squarely on the shoulders of the young management trainee under the direct guidance of the Consumer Sales Manager.

This expatriate boss proved to be perhaps Tony's first mentor, teaching him things that could not be learned in a classroom from Marketing to Finance. He read textbooks on his own and felt no shame in asking even subordinates for further explanation when he needed them. He taught Tony how to research on his own. It was an incredible opportunity, presenting the young executive with dozens of projects on which to do feasibility studies and exposed him to the many possibilities in the Ghanaian industrial landscape. Even technical proposals no more scared him, as he knew the right questions to ask.

Out of this, Tony helped in the lubricant business for BP, as consumer sales dealt a lot with lubricants; and to sell lubricants successfully, one needed to understand the technical aspects. The clients of this arm of the business were from mining companies, big buyers, and big users, and it was in BP's best interest to recommend various kinds of oils for various applications. All this helped Tony immensely.

From the onset, the plan was to do no more than 10 years at whichever company he would work with after his university studies. On reaching BP, he realised that there were people who had been in the company for many years and grown through the ranks, but Tony had a different vision for his life. His target was to then work for himself for another 10 years and hopefully save enough to then decide what he really wanted to do with his life.

Looking back at all the years where his father had people working for him, and they would go to Ghana Cement Works together, Tony realised that being the boss was far better. He knew which of the managers and which of the accountants they gave tips to, and who came home for loans and assistance. Surely, he would rather be in his father's shoes than the one receiving tips. Also, the kind of money being paid as salaries even then was not to his satisfaction. Coming from a family background where they were relatively comfortable, his sights were set even higher.

As is usually the case where outsiders are brought in to fill a role in a company, Tony had unwittingly ruffled feathers just by being employed. BP at the time had three layers of staff: management, supervisory staff, and junior staff. When Tony was recruited as a management trainee – he learned of this rancour much later – the supervisory staff felt one from among their ranks deserved the promotion. That perhaps explained why he faced that much hostility. People would not even speak to him. His first assignment was with the sales team, which was made up of supervisory staff, who were supposed to teach him the rudiments of the business. This made for some very frosty car rides. It was not uncommon to drive in silence for three or four hours.

In 1977, Tony wrote a report he will never forget. Part of his role was simply to write on what he saw. He went a step further to point out things that were wrong and suggested improvements. In this report, he noted that the "Goodbye" sign at a filling station came before the "Welcome" sign. Either nobody had noticed, or they thought it too trivial to make a big deal out of.

What had happened was that in 1974, Ghana changed overnight from driving on the left – as is the case in the United Kingdom and some other Commonwealth nations – to driving on the right to mirror the country's neighbours to the north, east, and west. This meant that the entrances of filling stations became exits and vice versa. To Tony, this was a simple thing to change, and he put it in his report.

However, the retail sales team did not take kindly to being publicly exposed by a young upstart in consumer sales.

While on his rotation with the Finance Department, he once more wrote a proposal in a report suggesting easier ways to handle petty cash. He had not passed this report to an assistant at the time to the Finance Manager. This assistant was quite upset with Tony for making him look bad, not choosing an informal discussion rather than going straight to the formality of a report. Nevertheless, this eye for detail impressed his bosses, who were able to trust him with more and more.

BP was a good training ground for Tony. He gained experience working in Accra, Tamale, Kumasi, and Takoradi. Five years into his job at BP, Tony's eyes began to wander in search of opportunities elsewhere.

While in Tamale, he tried his hands at rice farming, but the business folded without registering any profit. However, he fell back on his sales skills and resorted to trading harvested rice from other farmers, buying during the harvesting season, and selling during the lean season.

By the seventh year, he had collaborated with two friends in Accra, to form a company. They set up a restaurant, at Osu. Their initial success exceeded their own expectations.

InTakoradi, he identifiedwood products as an area of interest, especially asTakoradi lies within a timber enclave with lot of sawmills around. As one with an eye for ideas and business, Tony found his way into the wood business shortly after the restaurant had found its footing as a successful business.

While still in Takoradi, he saw some tongue and groove (T & G) work which really impressed him. He rented a place in Jamestown in Accra and got a truckload of T & G profile boards on credit from the owner of Hardwood Timber Products and later Chairman of Sekondi Hassacas Football Club, Edward Nartey, whom he had met and formed an acquaintance with upon moving to the Western Region.

During a return to Takoradi to negotiate a loan to buy more products, Tony saw a nicely finished wooden crate sitting in Edward's factory, and this impressed Tony. He formed a partnership with Andy, a friend who was also his neighbour, who had a degree in Art from the Kwame Nkrumah University of Science and Technology (KNUST) and was a talented woodworker. Andy spent days in the workshop converting raw pieces of wood into exquisite pieces of furniture and more, such as creating chandeliers out of wood.

In 1984, Tony acquired a stand at a local trade fair to display his wooden T & G pieces, crates, and Andy's wooden chandeliers at the Ghana Industrial Furniture and Woodworking Industry Exhibition (GIFEX). It would be his second time meeting a sitting head of state.

Flt Lt Jerry John Rawlings, who was walking through the exhibitions, was attracted by the wooden chandelier. He however balked at the price, but Tony quietly explained to him that a unique chandelier like that made from wood belonged in the stately rooms of places like the Osu Castle, the seat of government at the time. Flt Lt Rawlings just looked at Tony and turned away.

However, just like his fame spread in his locale with his short clip in the Information Services vans, Tony found his picture on the front page of the Daily Graphic talking to the Chairman of the Provisional National Defence Council (PNDC), Flt Lt Rawlings.

Maybe that boosted the footfall to this stand, but a few days later, a prospector approached and inspected the wooden crates. He liked what he saw. It turned out that before him stood the Production Manager for Coca-Cola in Ghana, and he had had trouble obtaining enough wooden crates. Tony smelled opportunity. He quickly agreed to work assiduously to meet the demand from Coca-Cola.

After the fair, he got carpenters from Accra Timber Market, Takoradi, and Kumasi, with each bringing dozens of other carpenters with him. Calculating man that he is, Tony also thought up a simple approach of breaking down the process so that qualified carpenters were no longer required. He would buy the wood from Takoradi or Kumasi, get it sawn to appropriate sizes, and bring it down to the Jamestown warehouse in knock-down form.

Using the new production line process, anyone who was handy with a hammer and could follow simple instructions could do his part and pass it on to the next until a full crate emerged at the end of the process. This proved so successful that he even rented a second warehouse in Alajo to meet increased orders.

That was how he set up Tropical Products, making wood products for industrial use. In the long term, Tony moved away from Coca-Cola and concentrated on Achimota Brewery Company, brewers of the ABC brand of beer, to make their wooden crates for them. He extended the product offering to include wooden broom and brush handles, as well as industrial pallets.

Even before reaching year 10 in BP, however, Tony had had enough and called it quits. He had been transferred from Takoradi back to Accra, working on his most challenging project yet. At the time, BP did not have a bunkering service, that is, the sale of fuel to ships and boats. Tony was tasked with this responsibility, setting it up from the bottom up. He lived in the Ambassador Hotel for the period that his accommodation was being sorted out, leaving his personal effects in his bungalow in Takoradi. Since he was setting up the office from scratch, he would leave for the office at 6:00 every morning and return at about 8:00 every night.

One day, however, Tony received word that his belongings in Takoradi had been moved out of the official residence and sent to a warehouse in Accra. His own boss had authorised this action. It turns out that Tony's replacement needed the residence, though this was not made clear to him. At the very least, had his nine years of service not earned him the right to be told that they were going into his home to pack him out? What hurt Tony most was that his boss, whom he confronted over the matter, saw nothing wrong with what Tony saw as gross disrespect.

In a huff, Tony handed in a resignation letter. The Managing Director was out of town at the time, so there was a waiting period for him to get back.

One night upon the MD's request, the Finance Director, tracked Tony down. Tony would not rescind his decision. Eventually, the MD got a face-to-face meeting. His trump card was to show Tony what plans BP had for him. To say that it was impressive would be an understatement. However, from somewhere deep within, Tony found the conviction to refuse.

And so, his time at BP came to an end prematurely. He was enticed by the prospect of oil marketing yet found himself identifying and assessing investment opportunities for the business. These skills would come in handy during the next phase of his life.

Now, Tony had a decision to make. Though the restaurant was never really a long-term option for him, it was all he had now. However, as it lasted, the operation of the restaurant had unearthed some cracks in the partnership. The plan was to make money. Beyond that, however, each had his own idea about what to do with the windfall. There was no written agreement and no business plan. While one partner wanted to buy a car, the other wanted to move into trade, etc. These problems took a toll on the personal relationships of the partners.

After a piece of business was conducted with the Ghana National Trading Corporation (GNTC), one partner collected the cheque and left to the UK with the full amount. Today, they laugh about it together, but at the time, Tony was naturally displeased.

The other partner's wife ran the restaurant, and the lack of clear separation between home and business affairs caused a rift. It would be the coup de grace that caused Tony to leave the business entirely. One day, Tony had asked to inspect the company accounts, which had not been well received. Rather than argue, Tony just went to his home at Kokomlemle and promised himself that he would never return. Tony was out. In the end, the partnership withered away. Another chapter in Tony's life story was closed.

He seamlessly moved to manage Tropical Products. In fact, business was so good that he had built a house from the profits of the business only three or four years after beginning production. The more exhibitions he attended, the wider his products also went.

In 1989, however, at just the age of 34, Tony was forced to consider the future of the timber industry and whether he wanted to remain in it. While exhibiting at GIFEX London, an environmental lobby came round protesting the use of tropical hardwood. He was now at a crossroads. He was ready to make a long-term investment, buying timber equipment to increase his production locally. Reasoning that the wood industry in the following 20 or 30 years could be problematic, he started to back out, looking for his next area of business.

More than five years had passed, and Tony was no closer to finding his flagship business. He had transitioned into Tropical Products, but the long-term future of the wood business was uncertain.

He decided to embark on post-graduate studies, arriving at the Ghana School of Law in 1987. He left with more than a law degree, having met Barbara, his would-be wife there. He passed out successfully and was called to the Ghana Bar – Tony Oteng-Gyasi, Esq.

The year 1989 held some more significance for him. This was when the government announced a 30-year plan to electrify the whole country in the national budget. Ever the avid reader, he pored over the budget in the national dailies and arrived at the conclusion that there would soon be boundless opportunities in the electrical industry.

Falling back on his skill set built up over his decade in BP and his half-decade of working for himself, he saw an opportunity in manufactured representation. He visited the trade sections at the British High Commission and the US Embassy looking for companies who were doing things in that area. Unfortunately, all the bigger companies, especially in Europe and the US, were already represented in Ghana, making it near impossible to break through.

Undeterred, he looked towards India on a recommendation from a player in the space during a reconnaissance trip to the UK. India was more favourable than China because of the English language. A subsequent visit to the Indian High Commission gave him the information he needed.

As though it was destiny, he was led into the office of an Indian gentleman named John Bawa in the trade section. They hit it off immediately on a professional level. Both were Roman Catholics, which only deepened the connection.

By the time Tony was leaving, he was armed with contacts in the Indian electrification industry, all of whom he began a correspondence with. However, as if to serve as a reminder that making it in business was an uphill task, he was met with rejections upon seeking contracts from the Utilities who were the generators and distributors of electricity in Ghana respectively. They were not used to products outside the traditional European and American sources.

Then, a fortuitous thing happened that very same year. The Indian government gave Ghana an Exim Bank of India credit line for about the equivalent of $10 million, on condition that the government could only use it to buy materials from India.

This forced the Utilities to open tenders to Indian suppliers. By this time, Tony had identified favourable business partners and was prepared. They went to the Indian High Commission to get a list of Indian companies that could supply transformers, cables, conductors, overhead lights, and hardware. John Bawa was the official they went through.

The company that Tony represented was one of the 10 that he gave to the Ghanaian officials, and at the end of the competitive tender, Tony's company won the largest contract of about $5 million. The feeling defied belief. He was on his way. When his first commission of $20,000 arrived, he just kept the banker's draft in his diary, occasionally staring at it and smiling. It would be another week before he deposited it at Social Security Bank (SSB), now Société General.

It could not have come at a better time. Though he had an exit plan in place at Tropical Products, business was slowing down faster than he had expected. The beer companies had teamed up and set up a company in Tema to produce plastic crates for them, taking away the beer market Tony had carefully cultivated. Left with just the soft drink market, he got Pepsi Cola on board, and also supplied wooden crates to Accra Breweries Limited (ABL).

For the pallets, he got procurement agencies and various warehouses in Tema but noticed that pallets made from tropical hardwood can last up to 20 years in warehouses. As he had predicted, the wood market was dying.

Tony, on the other hand, had breathed new life into his entrepreneurial dreams. Over the next four years, he won tender after tender, including World Bank bids. Though the Power utilities did not know that much about the Indian market, they used Tony's electrical suppliers and found them to be satisfactory. As a young man with an eye to the future, Tony saved all his commissions, going around town in his second-hand Nissan Sunny. Though Tropical Products was not what it once was, Tony began overland export, supplying wood to Togo and Benin, and in the process, squeezing the last bit of profit he could from his wood business.

When in 1991 a new MD was appointed for one of the Power utilities, Tony saw it as an opportunity to deepen his connection within the institution. He managed to get his partners in India to invite the new MD over to India for a familiarisation tour of their facilities. Tony believed in this kind of cultivation, from Heads of Engineering to MDs. Just like it was with John Bawa a few years earlier, the Roman Catholic connection played in Tony's favour when he went for an introductory visit.

In India, Tony learnt there were two big groups: The house of the Birlas and the house of the Tatas. They were the two big groups in constant competition, unseating each other as number one from time to time. CIMMCO International was the international trading division of the house of the Birlas, a huge conglomerate with factories for everything.

Tony's visit there with the MD was his first as well. He could not help feeling that the factory workers and the management were no better than Ghanaians. A seed was sown in his head: why could we not do this in Ghana?

It started as a dream to assemble transformers in Ghana. Around 1992 on one of his trips, he got one engineer from CIMMCO International to take him to a factory they bought transformers from and met the owner of the factory – the chairman – and his son – the MD. Tony and the MD got along well, especially since they were age mates. They discussed the assembly idea and agreed on it. They quickly drew up a business plan. The stumbling block, however, was the financing. Over $10 million was needed, pricing Tony out immediately.

His search for investment led him to a friend who was doing very well in the shea nut export business. After examining the business plan, Tony's friend passed it on to a foreign expert who was working at the Ministry of Finance. To Tony's disappointment, this consultant deemed the assembly of transformers an impossible undertaking in Ghana. None of Tony's justifications could change his mind. His friend promptly backed out of any investment.

The thing about transformers is that they can be complex to put together, looking at how each one is made up of hundreds of small parts. Still, Tony had an unwavering belief that with the right technology and equipment, it was possible. Without funding, however, the idea was dead on arrival. He thought of something simpler to do.

Tony has his curiosity and love for reading to thank for stumbling into his next course of action. Around Alajo in Accra, where he had rented a warehouse for making his crates, he had stopped one day to buy kelewele and found an interesting sheet of paper. Upon further inquiries from the kelewele seller, it turned out that another warehouse was being cleared out, having belonged to a former military-man-turned-industrialist who was forced into exile in 1979 during the Armed Forces Revolutionary Council (AFRC) era.

Hundreds of documents were thrown out of the warehouse during the clearing. As Tony passed by, he picked up some of them and discovered a company in the UK that sold business plans for between £70 and £150, indicating the equipment, cost implications, and raw materials needed. He contacted them and engaged their services a few times.

In the passage of time, the owner of the company in the UK passed away, and his daughter inherited it. She, however, decided to liquidate, so having seen Tony's name in their records, wrote to him and offered him the business plans. He bought so many of them that he read from time to time.

That was how cables came into the picture after the transformers business failed to take flight.

He had business plans for a small, medium, and large cable company, how many tonnes of material he would need, what kinds of equipment was required, and so on. Through his investment of time into studying business plans, he became so adept at it that he could develop skeletal plans on the back of an envelope by himself to see if the numbers were right.

Still, he got further training through the EMPRETEC programme for training entrepreneurs. Alan Kyerematen, the present-day Minister of Trade and Industry, the then Director of the programme, and a former colleague in Legon, managed to influence him to attend and learn even more about business plans.

Through his contacts from the training, he was put in touch with some consultants who helped him to draw up a commercial business plan for a cable and conductors' business in Ghana. Tony could not believe how good the numbers were looking. He went back to EMPRETEC, requesting a technical and feasibility plan. This time, another consultant named Kwasi Poku and his team managed to get relevant industry information. The numbers were not as rosy as the commercial plan, but they were still very impressive. Nothing would stop Tony at this point.

Funding was still the major hurdle. Because he was looking to raise a couple of million dollars, he wrote to various manufacturers of cable-making equipment around the world to try and find supplier's credit.

Once more, he took a trip to the UK, and then took on a spur-of-the-moment decision to visit Belgium to see a company he had been corresponding with on equipment. The MD was a man named Leopold.

Leopold's employee gave Tony a factory tour and showed him the range of equipment they manufacture. Over lunch with Leopold, Tony broached the subject of funding, requesting part-payment and supplier's credit. Leopold flatly refused. No argument was convincing enough.

In the end, the employee drove Tony back to the airport, about an hour's drive away. Tony had a last-ditch pitch. He left a copy of his business plan for Leopold to examine. With any luck, he would see that there was money to be made.

Maybe it was Tony's broad knowledge that warmed the employee's heart or their joint passion for football. Whatever it was, it must have left an impression because a few months later, this man informed Tony that Leopold was on his way to Cote d'Ivoire to install some equipment. He would try to convince Leopold to make a stop in Ghana.

Leopold followed up with a call, indicating that he was merely coming on a casual visit, and not on business. Tony was fine with that. He picked him up on a Friday at the airport and booked him into Labadi Beach Hotel for the night. On Saturday, he took him to the National Museum, Independence Square, Aburi, and his home at Achimota. They had lunch on Sunday afternoon and in the evening, Tony took him back to the airport to catch his flight.

In all this time together, they never talked about Tony's proposal. A few months later, Leopold called Tony to say he had been thinking about the proposal. He was on another trip, this time to Nigeria to sell some equipment, he passed through Ghana, and after discussing numbers, they signed a Memorandum of Understanding (MOU).

He had taken Leopold to see a parcel of industrial land in Tema that he had acquired previously. This was the site for Tropical Cable & Conductor Limited. Once more, Leopold showed scepticism that this bare land could be a factory. With the assurance from Tony that it would be completed in nine months and the MOU signed, Leopold left Ghana satisfied.

The terms of the MOU favoured the Belgian heavily. Tony would have to make a huge advance payment, based on nothing more than trust. As an indication of how much faith he had in his business plan – or how desperate he was – Tony sent the money. It was his entire life savings.

With the money paid, the ball was rolling. The work on the factory began. A mistake Tony made was to tell the contractor how much money was available for the building. Unfortunately, the contractor cut a lot of corners, and to this day, though they remain friends, Tony has never given the contractor another job to do for him. He had broken Tony's trust.

With his tireless work ethic, the dream was taking shape. Banks in the 1980s and 1990s in Ghana were not set up for industry. In fact, starting with a loan might have been detrimental to the business, with interest rates easily hitting 40%. By all his projections, even getting a loan at the lowest available rate would doom the project. That was why he sought supplier's credit and used personal finances.

A few years prior, he applied for a loan to establish a nail-making factory, even buying and rehabilitating used equipment. In the end, the application was rejected because he did not have sufficient collateral, and the bank insisted that he would use the money to finish building his house, which was under construction.

Today, the business climate is slightly better. Banks are only willing to support entrepreneurs with a record of accomplishment, however. Tony can understand them:

"Too many of our entrepreneurs do not look completely at the project. Personally, I have given money out to friends and relations trying to start a business and invariably I have found out that I have lost most of it. People's attitude to starting a business is not right. When you start a business, you need to get your priorities right. I have seen business plans with two saloon cars right from the beginning. Our people need to distinguish between money which is essential and money for ancillary activities. Too many of our start-ups do not think that way. I don't know whether it's a lack of training."

It is not surprising that Tony thinks this way. When building Tropical Cable, he did not even think about office space. Every cedi was pumped into the factory. The compound was unpaved for the first four years These are lessons picked up from expatriates who come to Ghana, get into manufacturing, and do very well. When he was in the wooden crates business at Alajo, an Indian in a neighbouring warehouse stocked second-hand equipment from his home country.

This man began manufacturing yellow car dusters onsite. Anything which was not required essentially for the business, he considered a luxury. His office was just an area cordoned off with plywood. It was only after striking it rich that he allowed himself a few luxuries.

After the Tropical Cables factory was built, the real work began. The only people Tony wanted to recruit were professionals skilled in manufacturing cables. To him, everyone else was merely supporting staff. He employed a former engineer from a multinational cable manufacturer. Through him, five other engineers and technicians also joined.

To start with, there was no accountant. Mr T. V. A. Mensah was a friend from secondary school and a chartered accountant. His advice to Tony was to get an accounts clerk who could write the vouchers, and occasionally he would come and work on the books. He joined much later as the Director of Finance and even though currently retired is still a member of the Board. Three months later, he augmented the accounting clerk with affordable accounting software from SoftTribe for about $1,500. For the size of the business, that was enough to start with. They bought a desktop computer, installed the software, and worked.

Tony was in the trenches with his people. Duty demanded it. He was never scared to get his hands dirty. His was not a multinational starting a subsidiary. This was from the ground up.

The ready market for his cables and conductors were the Power Utilities, though there was no guarantee that they would buy his products. Indeed, for the first six months of production, they did not. There were processes that needed to be completed, like getting certification from the

Ghana Standards Board (GSB) – now Authority. Getting this certification meant going to sit in their office to get tests done, a process that could really drag. Tony was ready to make a bother of himself.

Finally, he got his tests done and his products certified. The Utilities were satisfied. When it came to pricing, he agreed that they should pay him whatever they were paying for imports. In the end, he got a contract, largely because they felt the need to support local industries.

Approval was one thing. Getting the order was another altogether. The frustrations in the system were getting to Tony, but he had come too far to quit. For months, he was chasing for a contract.

One day, his British Executive Service Overseas (BESO) consultant, Tom Bonikowski, came to visit. He got an idea seeing his European consultant in front of him. He asked Tom to wear a suit and follow him to the utility. Tom would just need to sit pretty while Tony did the talking. Upon getting there, Tony introduced Tom as his boss who had come to Ghana in anticipation of the order. It was done that same day. While disappointed by the attitude of his fellow Ghanaians, Tony used it to his advantage. It was not the last time he would use Tom to expedite a process, presenting him as the overall boss.

Tropical Cable & Conductor Limited grew from strength to strength. Most people just see the success and not the sweat. For Tony, entrepreneurship was a journey, and not a singular effort. He knew there would be ups and downs.

There is a failed supermarket that he started. The memory keeps him grounded.

Not everything he touched turned to gold. He was more than ready to encounter tough times. What he would not do, though, would be to learn nothing from his mistakes and repeat them. His penchant to learn from failures rather than waste time on regret kept him well.

While he did not like it, Tony also got used to the Ghanaian tax regime, where there was a plethora of pre-production taxes, from import duty paid on imported raw materials to Value Added Tax (VAT) on production materials. Even before an item has been produced, tax is paid on it, serving as a huge disincentive for future entrepreneurs.

With more than half a century of life under his belt, Tony can look back and see some things about himself: he was born for this. He just cannot see how it would work if he had gone through the ranks at BP or moved elsewhere. He loves the risk. He notes how nothing can hold him back when he has made up his mind about something, not even a thought about how his wife and children would survive.

Tony still bets heavily on himself. He spent $8 million on a new factory, believing that he would make that money back. Any money he has in savings is not there to accumulate. For example, when an Investment House tried to convince him to invest in their new equity mutual fund because he had money invested there, he declined, knowing that that money was for his factory. Today, the factory's profits have far outstripped any investment instrument he could have left his money in.

Though he did not grow up deprived, he learned from an early age that postponed consumption held more value than eating all of one's seeds before the planting season. He never compared himself to anyone and was more likely to spend time in reading and preparation than to make a splash trying to impress anyone.

The walk of an entrepreneur can be all-consuming. For those who make it to the top, it can be lonely. However, there is something in them that keeps calling them to go once more. For those they love, they can bear the brunt of feeling like they are in second place.

In talking to Barbara Oteng-Gyasi, married to Tony since 1995 after meeting in the late 1980s in law school, she has had to adapt to her husband. She has had to get used to knowing that he would forget about many things on the domestic front. She has learned not to get angry when he does not run his riskiest moves past her, knowing that as the more pragmatic of the two, she would likely rein him in. (On the other hand, he is quick to apologise when she is proved right about a wrong decision he made). She comforts herself in knowing that he trusts her judgment completely, and he knows she can cut through all the fat to get to the meat of any matter.

When he recoils in his shell because he is internalising his problems, Barbara gives him the space he needs to brood. Where she can get him to talk, she will, but there are times when he has heavy things to deal with.

There was a time where someone got electrocuted in the factory. Another time, a bus accident claimed the life of one staff. His doting wife was able to get to him to understand that there was not much he could have done to prevent these things.

Tony Oteng-Gyasi's curiosity has opened more doors for him down the line than he could ever imagine. He has scaled heights that few will ever be able to. And yet, he remains hungry, wondering what is next for him on his entrepreneurial journey. It can only get better. It always does.

CASE STUDY TWO

LETICIA OSAFO- ADDO

CHAPTER 3

THE MAGIC OF THE PEPPER SEED

LETICIA OSAFO-ADDO

"Never give up on a dream just because of the time it will take to accomplish it."

Leticia Osafo-Addo can afford to smile. Her story is one of the best known in Africa, told many times over in local tabloids and international pages, as well as on television and in social media. Her hot chilli sauce, popular in Ghana and eaten with most dishes, sells all over the world.

But looking at the business now is to belie its shaky beginnings. Like many start-up businesses that kick off with little or no capital, the now-CEO of Samba Foods started her company with only 10 dollars. "Yes, I had only ten US dollars when I decided to start this business. I had no business plan and knew nothing about the food business. All I know is that my mind was just made up to make shitor," she recalls.

After a sojourn in Germany for many years, Leticia Osafo-Addo returned to the land of her birth with a family and solid experience in nursing, but no clear picture of what the future held for her. However, she was not worried. Hers had been a life of constant change for as long as she could remember.

From the beginning of her life, she was put in a position to see the path and lead the way. As the first of seven children, Leticia was born on 19th February 1952 on the University of Science and Technology (UST) campus, Kumasi, to Mr and Mrs J E Kwarteng.

Despite her middle-class upbringing, Leticia did not have things as smooth sailing as she would have liked. While her siblings got to go to the more prestigious University Primary School, she started at Weweso Local Authority Primary School. When she wrote her Common Entrance Examination in Form Two, she got admission into Mfantsiman Girls' Secondary School. The problem was that she was the last person to know about it. She was not even aware that she had passed the exam.

Eventually, St Mary's Secondary School wrote to her, indicating that since she did not turn up to register at Mfantsiman, her spot was given to somebody else, and her details were sent to St Mary's. Unfortunately, the letter from St Mary's also arrived after the deadline, which made things even more confusing for young Leticia.

She ended up at T. I. Ahmadiyya Secondary School in Kumasi. Two years later, Leticia was on the move again. By the time she had enrolled at University Secondary School – which is KNUST Senior High School today – she was used to the skipping around. It was here that she ended up writing her O-Level exams.

Afterwards, once more, Leticia was on the move. This time, her travels would lead her beyond the shores of Ghana. After missing out on educational opportunities in Saltpond and Accra, she would not be denied this time; she was on her way to Germany.

This was 1969, where Ghanaians of all social classes had made their home in different European countries. Leticia's uncle had told her in advance of her exams that if she could only pass her O-Levels, he would sponsor her education in whichever field she was interested in in Germany.

Her best bet as a steppingstone was nursing school. In those days, scholarships were freely available for nursing students. With her fees being paid, Leticia had the peace of mind to concentrate on her studies. The European leg of her life had begun.

Sitting in the German city of Monchengladbach that November, in her mind, her youth ended. Everything was so foreign to her. She had to begin thinking about the future.

What she saw as a gateway to other things would quickly become a passion. It helped that she was doing well.

After completing her general nursing course in 1973, she sought further opportunities. That came in the form of specialist nursing in intensive care therapy and anaesthesia for another three years in Dusseldorf and Krefeld respectively.

On the personal side of things, Leticia's life was changing. She had fallen in love with a Ghanaian young man, Dr Kofi Osafo-Addo, and was just settling into life as a dutiful wife when her husband brought things to a screeching halt. His desire was for her to stay home to raise their children, and as an internist, he certainly had the means to care for a single-income household.

After 25 years in Germany, the Osafo-Addos made the decision to return to Ghana. They would be arriving in Accra in 1984 to a totally different world from the one that she had left. After years of political instability, the country had settled into relative calm since the military government of the Provisional National Defence Council (PNDC) came to power at the end of 1981.

Their journey to Ghana had taken them through London, where they stayed for a little while. Leticia's uncles questioned the wisdom in her husband's decision to come back to Ghana at that time. Yet, he was insistent. He wanted to go home.

Acclimatising to life in Ghana did not come without its challenges. Dr Osafo-Addo was initially employed at the UST Hospital in Kumasi, before being transferred to the

Tetteh Quarshie Memorial Hospital in Mampong. At each stop, he moved with the whole family. As the children grew up and had to enter the school system, change was on the horizon again, since on the Akwapim Ridge in the 1990s, there was not a school that the young couple found satisfactory enough for their little scholars.

At this time, Leticia's husband took a detour into private practice and moved the family for the last time toTema in the Greater Accra Region. For the first time in many years, Leticia felt alone. This was a strange feeling because she was not one to feel uncomfortable being by herself. After dropping the children off at SOS Hermann Gmeiner School and her husband went to work, she was left alone with her thoughts.

She looked back at all the different phases of her life and thought that she was ready for another one, this time, determined by what she wanted. Circumstances had forced decisions on her, and even though she learned to enjoy them, she was ready to this time forge a path for herself and take her own destiny in her hands.

She decided to put her medical skills to use. This led her to Dawhenya, where she set up a small outpatient clinic.

The town of Dawhenya in the Ningo-Prampram District of the Greater Accra Region is noted for West Africa's largest irrigation scheme, with over seven million acres under irrigation.

A Baptism of Pepper

Never one to sit idly, Leticia's restlessness kicked in. She took advantage of the agricultural economy around her clinic and went into pepper cultivation. She started with only one acre after an acquaintance of hers had harassed her to give farming a try. At harvest time, she had some kilogrammes of pepper. While it served as an inspiration to go through a second growing season, she asked herself, "What am I going to do with all this pepper?"

The year 1993 opened another chapter in Leticia's life. She did not know it at the time, but her life's work was finally taking shape. Every experience in her life to that point had prepared her for this moment, even though she was unaware of how big her next decision would be.

Up to that point, nobody bottled and sold shitor, a locally made pepper sauce that consists of pepper, shrimps, oil and other spices. It had always been a staple that students took to boarding school with them. For generations, it had been a mainstay in Ghanaian kitchens, mostly made to last several meals.

Staring at all her powdered pepper, an idea seized control of Leticia. She embarked on a little bit of market research and discovered that you could not just walk up to a supermarket and pick up a jar of shitor. Her excitement was palpable as she discussed the idea with her husband. Their conclusion was to give it a try, and with that, Samba Foods was born.

There was no business plan. There were no projections on spreadsheets. There was only opportunity. She seized it and has never looked back.

From the medical field to being a stay-at-home-mom to farming and now entrepreneurship, Leticia's metamorphosis was an interesting journey to self-actualisation. Her definition of an entrepreneur was simple: a person who translates a business idea into a venture that can make money. All she had was an idea and the will to not give up.

Skill Development

Years later, when she did the Empretec training course for budding entrepreneurs as part of the 23rd batch, the director of Empretec Ghana at the time, the late Kweku Hutchful, noted her noticeable persistence. After a competency test for all participants, he announced, "If this lady says she wants the brown one, please give her the brown one."

To date, Empretec Ghana has trained thousands of entrepreneurs, removing the focus from just financial support and technical skills training, but working on the attitude of the entrepreneur.

"What turned me into a businesswoman is the entrepreneurship training I received from Empretec Ghana," Leticia noted. Anybody who had known Leticia from her childhood could easily have predicted her rise through entrepreneurship. "I sold everything under the sun," she said. Indeed, whether it was selling milk toffees – popularly called "ayigbe toffee" – as a 12-year-old schoolgirl, or selling rice when she was in Form Three, or even going to the Ayigya market in Kumasi to sell cassava during school vacations, she was quietly sharpening her abilities in sales.

Perhaps her later endeavour at farming came from short job stints in the offices of the university farms belonging to the Faculty of Agriculture at the Kwame Nkrumah University of Science and Technology (KNUST).

In the four months between writing her O-Levels and departing for Germany, Leticia poured her heart and soul into her mother's business, growing it exponentially in such a short time. By her own admission, she was a hard worker. In later reflections, she pointed out that she picked up the entrepreneurial spirit from her mother's modest business and her father's penchant for discipline.

As the firstborn, she had to be hard working. As a woman, she felt that she had to work even twice as hard to get the results she wanted. In her home, she had three brothers born in a row after her in an era where boys spent their time playing while girls did the housework and cooking. The onus lay on her to ensure the house was well kept. Leticia was ready to brave austere conditions to get the results she wanted.

When they lived in the university quarters in her youth, all she had in her room was a small table and a small bed. Though people would come through the room many times in a day, she always kept it tidy, straightening the bed as soon as someone sitting on it got up. Her principled ways could get irritating, but she knew they were always appreciated. From washing and ironing for her father on Saturdays to cleaning the house from top to bottom, there was always something to do.

Her first try at formal leadership, though, was as Girls' Prefect in Form Five of secondary school. These leadership skills were further honed during her sojourn in Germany. Later in life, people who experienced her no-nonsense approach to work, her prim and proper ways, and her strict faithfulness to time nicknamed her Angela Merkel after the German Chancellor who is renowned for her no-nonsense approach to things.

Thus, it was no wonder that Leticia was ready to bear the risks that came with starting an industry that did not exist up to that point.

It helped that she possessed a personality to not take no for an answer, a perfectionist with a passion to excel. With role models like Prime Ministers MargaretThatcher of the United Kingdom, Golda Meir of Israel, and Indira Gandhi of India, her sights were set to greater things.

On the local front, she took inspiration from Esther Ocloo, a pioneering Ghanaian female entrepreneur and industrialist who established Women's World Banking for women to obtain microcredit facilities and more specifically to her interests, Nkulenu Industries, a leading food-processing company at the time in Ghana.

Of Women and Entrepreneurship

As every business does, Leticia experienced challenges, some bigger than others. She expected it. As time went on, the enterprise grew. Sales were going according to her expectation, and she was ready to expand Samba Foods. That was when an Australian company she identified as a potential partner soured the experience for her. The long and short of it was that Leticia took out a loan for the company, the partnership fell through, and she was left holding the ball. No amount of negotiation with the bank in question worked. She had to pay back the loan and its accrued interest without any reprieve. For her, that was the end of her association with banks.

In fact, for an entrepreneur, Leticia developed a strange relationship with debt. She avoids it as much as she can. And while time has made her worry less about debt and unexpected costs like trucks and machines breaking down, she remembers how these used to keep her up at night. Perhaps her having started from little accounted for this, to the extent that at a point, she would take a taxi to work for a period rather than acquire a new car.

Being a woman in business also comes with its peculiar challenges. While historically, Ghanaian women have been entrepreneurs, the reality is that at certain levels of business, it is a male-dominated field. Despite rising to the top over many years of hard work, not too long ago, her ideas at the table had to be outstanding before anybody would even listen to what she had to say.

Unless women are strong, this could very easily chip away at their self-confidence. That added pressure of always having to be excellent before any credit is given has worn out many a woman. Leticia had her moments where she was made to feel every bit the woman in the room.

This is even before considering that the female entrepreneur could very well be wearing a minimum of three hats as was the case with Leticia: mother, wife, business owner. Each of these placed incessant demands on her which made her assume the position of a superwoman, while at the same time, trying to outperform men who are not saddled with similar demands on their time. There was a time when she had her husband, mother, and sister all sick at home, and at the same time trying to make Samba Foods thrive.

On top of all these, many successful women have had negative insinuations cast upon them, some of which have been near impossible to ever shake off.

"When I decided to start the business, I became a subject of ridicule. People found it very demeaning for a trained medical professional like myself who had spent several years training overseas, to sell 'ordinary' pepper sauce," she explained. Fortunately, for Leticia, her strong science background gave her confidence to articulate ideas when it came to nutrition and on subject matters within the food processing and preservation industry. Whether in a room full of investors or bankers, she has not allowed fear to stop her from getting what she wants.

And Lady Luck has indeed smiled on Leticia. Growth has been slower than she would have liked, but it has been steady and upward. She learned to be patient to allow the success to come. After all, she was building an industry from the ground up. She was ready to play the long game, trading short-term success for a seat at the table of entrepreneurial giants.

Competition

Soon, competition started springing up from individuals and established companies as well. Bottled shitor lined shelves of supermarkets and small corner shops all over the country. Even Unilever got in on the act for a few years with Royco Shitor Mix. Deep down inside, it was validation for her. Shitor in jars was a game-changer. She had built a great product, and now established companies wanted a piece of the pie.

Leticia still takes pride in her journey and her product. She stands on three pillars she believes have made her successful: the quality and consistency of the product, the availability of the product, and the price of the product. These have led her to innovate and go a step further. From shitor in jars, she went on to produce non-spooning shitor options. Her shitor in sachets proved to be a boost for fast-food establishments in Ghana, including Chicken Inn, Pizza Inn, Palace Mall, and KFC.

Today, Leticia can now laugh about some of the ridicule that was shot her way in the 1990s. Her decision to return to Ghana had spawned wagging tongues about how she went abroad to come and prepare shitor in Ghana. At the time, however, those words would demoralise her completely. Needless to say, she has developed thicker skin today.

Expansion

By 1996, Leticia knew she had to improve on herself if she was to take her business to the level she believed it could reach. She completed a two-year MBA in Management Technology and Innovation from Wageningen Agricultural University, in The Netherlands. She also got a diploma in Quality Assurance and Marketing in Food Processing from the International Agricultural Centre, also in Wageningen.

Armed with her new knowledge, she felt equipped to be able to make some changes.

After having tasted success in shitor production, rather than look for other businesses to try, Leticia decided to expand Samba Foods' product line.

She diversified into groundnut processing and packaging. The company's groundnut processing plant, probably the largest in West Africa, is testament to how much her hard work has paid off. From her factory, she makes bulk groundnut paste for Cocoa Processing Company's Choco Delight chocolate spread. She also makes ginger-garlic paste, garlic paste and kpakpo shitor sauce, fruit jam, egushie powder and more. Samba Shitor remains the flagship product, however.

The company has been expanded to include large scale groundnut processing and shitor for clients like the UNHCR, Ghana Armed Forces Supply Depot, Volta Aluminium Company (VALCO), Cocoa Processing Company, and Unilever among others.

With time, her intention is to have an academy to train young people in food production, processing, and preservation. Her dream is to change the mindsets of government and young people on the importance of training and working with one's hands. As an appointed role-model ambassador for Technical and Vocational Education and Training (TVET) in Ghana, Leticia has seen the need to empower the youth with skills. As an industrialist, Leticia has seen how value addition to a young person's life by learning a trade and excelling in it can impact not just them and their families, but whole communities.

Still, food processing and preservation is her primary business.

Samba Foods has come a long way since its inception. From the very beginning, there was hardly any real corporate structure to the business. Aside starting without a business plan, financial records were not a priority. Though this has changed today, and she does proper analysis of her financials, she still trusts her instincts and intuition with a healthy dose of scepticism, where necessary. Better from a Bitter Bank Experience.

When she would run low on operating cash, she simply bartered with suppliers, giving them shitor in exchange for household items like tomato paste. In the early years, these included Multi Stores and Ghana National Trading Corporation (GNTC), who would negotiate supplier's credit with Leticia. At one point, Multi Stores had to import glass jars on behalf of Samba Foods.

From her bad experience with banks, Leticia has found ways around the banking system, even requesting clients to pre-finance orders – up to even 70%.

Samba Foods continues to rise above major hurdles. While the supply chain for shitor has been established with the availability of pepper and onions, the groundnut side of things was once unable to supply clients on a consistent basis. For instance, a client requested about 120 tonnes of groundnut a month. That represents about 1,000 bags. Unable to get anything close to that figure – even when trying to augment produce from Gambia and Senegal – it presented a major hurdle to growth.

This dire situation resulted in groundnuts being imported from Brazil to keep the business. She also had a client in Belgium requiring one container monthly, but unfortunately, she was unable to meet even 10% of the demand. This had to do with groundnuts being susceptible to aflatoxin infection, meaning that they fail quality tests regularly and cannot be exported.

To get around this, Leticia worked with the Rural Enterprises Project for support in acquiring a buying centre and semi-processing facility in Tamale, since most of the producers are in the northern part of Ghana. That means that now, they buy the whole groundnuts, deshell, sort, and grade at source, before sending to Tema, where the factory is.

By outsourcing this, she does not have to deal with having to sort through the adulterations mixed with the groundnuts at the farm gate.

Sadly, many Ghanaian entrepreneurs have lamented about a lack of trust for employees. Stories of betrayal could fill whole volumes. Leticia's tale is no different, even at a point forcing her to entrust Asian managers with her operations because of a proven track record of discipline, hard work and honesty. These are qualities she searches for in every employee.

Pain and Pride

Over the course of time, though, recounting solutions has made Leticia smile. She wears her scars with pride. Remembering contracts signed and targets achieved makes her happy. Now, these painful points in her business life and long processes are all situations she feels proud to have come out of in one piece. However, in the moment, it was never that glamorous.

"I have given up many times," she reveals, "but the success or recognition that comes from persevering cancels out all the challenges."

Perseverance and persistence. These are two traits Leticia believes got her through many a predicament. In fact, she believes no entrepreneur can survive without these in generous measure.

She learnt not to cry over spilt milk and would always move forward. The past is the past. Not forgotten, but past.

When Samba Foods was listed on the Ghana Alternative Market in 2015, it was the culmination of decades of hard work, mistakes overcome and risks that went her way. Leticia could not be prouder of how far she had come.

A trophy-laden cabinet in her office tells a story of toil and triumph. Climbing the podium to get each one has fuelled an untameable spirit that has spurred her on. Behind the smiles, beyond the speeches, there lies suffering and pain. In that moment, it all dissolves. These too have become part of the Leticia Osafo-Addo story.

She has been awarded one of the highest national honours for civilians, the Order of the Volta, by the late President John Evans Atta Mills in 2011. She won Chartered Institute of Marketing (Ghana) Marketing Woman of the Year in 2001, and Highly Commendable Businesswoman in Africa at the 2006 African Investor Awards. She won at the 2010 Builders of African Economies in Abidjan, an award won previously by African titans of business-like Mike Adenuga Jr and Mo Ibrahim. These awards, no matter when they were won, serve as daily motivation to keep striving.

She has served on the councils of the Ghana Stock Exchange and the Association of Ghana Industries among many others. She has joined government delegations to Brazil, South Africa, the United Kingdom and more. And she has won countless personal and product awards for her work with Samba Foods. Today, Leticia may not be the nurse she trained to be, but she sees that her focus has changed from healing to preventing disease through good nutrition. Hers has been a life of change and adapting to change. That, perhaps, has been the one constant in her journey, but she has enjoyed every moment.

The 2020 Entrepreneurs Foundation of Ghana Female Entrepreneur of the Decade has still got more left in her. She dreamt big, started small, and adapted at every step of her path. Is she done? No. In fact, she cannot wait to see where the next change will lead her.

CASE STUDY THREE

GWYNETH GYIMAH ADDO

CHAPTER 4

DARE TO BE DIFFERENT

GWYNETH GYIMAH ADDO

"Passion is the genesis of genius"

Anthony H. Robbins

The global human hair industry, by some estimates, is worth over $7 billion, and is expected to top $10 billion by 2024.

Directing affairs from her worldwide headquarters in Accra, Ghana, Gwyneth Gyimah Addo is making her mark on an industry that is showing no signs of slowing down. Between managing family and running an expanding beauty empire, Gwyneth wears many hats.

What started it – and remains the jewel in the crown – is Hair Senta, a side hustle that had its roots in the boot of a car before becoming what it is today, one of the most easily recognised names when it comes to hair for any occasion, preference, and budget.

From an initial investment of the equivalent of $20,000 going up in smoke, the story of this successful homegrown enterprise meanders its way through a bank, a foreign trip, and many paths littered with sweat and tears. Many, many tears.

For one who believes that entrepreneurs are made and not born, Gwyneth most likely won the genetic lottery when it comes to business. "I inherited the entrepreneurial spirit from my Ashanti father, and trading ability from my mum, a Kwahu," Gwyneth says with a laugh.

While still only a little girl in Class One, Gwyneth had the presence of mind to put cooked oats in polythene bags and sold them with milk powder and bread to her classmates. Unbeknownst to her, she was getting her entrepreneurial feet wet the same way many successful people before her had, by finding or creating opportunity. She fell in love with it immediately.

By Class Five, she was organising dances for friends where she collected a token from anyone who wanted to attend, a role she reprised organising parties for friends while studying at Akosombo International School (AIS) and later at the University of Ghana – finding time between heavy reading assignments in literature and philosophy. She was coming into her own as a salesperson, enjoying bringing people together and picking up skills that she would need to come naturally to her by the time she became a business owner.

Family is very important to Gwyneth. Born to Charles Allen Gyimah and Susana Osei Nyarko in 1982, her parents have had her back from the very beginning.

Their home in Laterbiokorshie in Accra was filled with laughter and joy. As an innovator himself, Gwyneth's father spoke into her life. She can still hear him say, "Ɛnsɛsɛ wobɛyɛ akwadworɔ," (Translation: You shouldn't be lazy) whenever she was letting her standards slip. He was Gwyneth's first influence.

Gwyneth's mother did a lot of the legwork in the nascent stages of Hair Senta, going door-to-door trying to make sales. One of her brothers designed the logos, and another has made it his personal responsibility to ensure she does not get complacent.

Gwyneth's first dream was to follow in her maternal grandfather's footsteps and become a lawyer. Life had other ideas. She was privileged enough to do her national service at Standard Chartered Bank. Her positive work ethic led to her gaining a permanent position at the end of the one year. That is how between 2006 and 2012 she worked as a credit analyst, responsible for working on clients' portfolios and structuring ways to provide credit facilities suited for them.

After leaving the bank in 2012, her next step was an MBA in Entrepreneurship and Innovation from China Europe International Business School (CEIBS). As fate would have it, she was awarded the Most Promising Female Entrepreneur of the Year some years after graduating as recognition for her translating the concepts learnt in the classroom into real life success.

Through a maze of events, Hair Senta and its associated companies were birthed. While Gwyneth may smile about the outcome and be optimistic about what is to come, the journey to the present was anything but straightforward.

It probably should come as no surprise that Gwyneth was able to find success. She always had a bit of a streak in her that drove her to do the things she wanted to do. Entrepreneurs are risk-takers. Even rule breakers. And Gwyneth broke the rules if they got in the way of her happiness.

Girls in AIS were not allowed to perm their hair or apply makeup. Not Gwyneth. She strutted around campus with a perm and a layer of makeup. Perhaps her spirit was already pointing her to the beauty industry subconsciously. Beauty was such a huge part of her identity that she just could not help it.

Maybe her decision to defy the authorities in AIS stemmed from a point of pain. At the age of eight, she had so little hair. She was constantly laughed at. Hairpieces would be her saving grace in her adult years. She could do as she pleased with her hair.

There is no single one-size-fits-all motivation to start a business. For Gwyneth, it was a hint of desperation. Despite her love for beauty, her hair just would not cooperate. It may have seemed relatively longer in the regimented environment of a Ghanaian secondary school, but with the restrictions removed, she just was not where she wanted to be regarding hair.

However, the entrepreneur in her saw not only opportunities to beautify herself, but also to make some money out of it. A quick glance around her led her to conclude that many other women suffered in silence about their lack of hair. As she solved her personal problem, she could solve others' as well.

That is how in 2008, she got to selling hair extensions to close friends of hers. She would buy six pieces, keep two, and sell two each to two of them. While in the bank, she would get women who were interested in hair extensions and show them her samples. It normally took about six weeks to sell. Gwyneth was undeterred. She upped her quantities to 10. Those took longer to sell, but eventually, they were gone. She was inspired. It was time to get serious about hair.

And then in 2009, Gwyneth got her first real capital injection. It was a sum of $20,000 from her then fiancé, Charles Addo, who is now her husband. There was no turning back.

Deep down, she felt she had arrived. Other people she knew did not have access to sums like this. She was being given a massive head start and was going to take full advantage of it.

In order to maximise the investment, she financed her return ticket herself and spent $19,900 on hairpieces that she packed into suitcases and brought back to Ghana. The last $100 she spent on a tip to a group who helped her.

It did not take Gwyneth long to discover that her efforts would end in disaster. She learned a big lesson the hard way that scaling up was not just a question of increasing quantity. "I had bought rubbish," she recounted. "Proper rubbish."

What had worked when selling 10 hairpieces would not work when selling thousands of dollars' worth of products. In her haste to launch her hair business, Gwyneth had done no market research. Just as she had done with the single hairpieces, she bought what would suit her. Over the years, she would learn that business did not revolve around her tastes. Her first real dip into the deep end was the wakeup call she needed.

Even the marketing strategy needed to change. Loading the hairpieces into her car boot and attracting buyers at lunchtime while maintaining her bank job was just not enough. Many would pick a few pieces, look at them, and just drop them.

Gwyneth's mother took to shopping the hairpieces to salons on weekdays while Gwyneth was at work, and she herself would take over on weekends and when she went on leave.

Back in 2009, she could not afford a shop. The hair still needed to be sold. She tried selling from her car boot. Anxiety took mother and daughter to salons as far away as Kumasi to try to sell some of the hairpieces.

Their tenacity paid off somewhat. First Choice Hair & Beauty Salon bought GHS 1,000 worth of hair, which at the time was worth in the region of $1,000. Though insignificant, Faustina Adofo Adjagar, the owner of First Choice, gave Gwyneth hope. And that was what she badly needed at the time. Hope.

The harm had already been done. Gwyneth's family was disappointed in the poor quality of hair she had brought, and the fact that there were just a few buyers only compounded the negative feelings. Still, what was needed was for it to sell, so they rallied together to ensure the business did not die before it could be given a chance. To Gwyneth, it only cemented her belief that family was everything. Their support, combined with her passion, stoked a fire that could not be easily quenched.

That is why she tells entrepreneurs everywhere to have passion, because where the economy, friends, and even family – though not in her case – were to fail, the passion would help to ride the bad times. This personal vision of where one wants to go could be the only thing keeping the lights on in the business where every logical metric is screaming for the business owner to quit.

She could see that women in the bank wanted to look beautiful. Her friends wanted to look beautiful as well. So, even though this first foray into business would ultimately prove to be a failure, she felt that with the right changes, she could be back in business. "Nobody wants to just take a shower and show up," Gwyneth would remind herself. She was all in. It was at that point that she told herself that the beauty industry was one she was ready to throw all her chips into. After all, is business not about solving problems? Once the entrepreneur's aim is to solve problems and finds these solutions, the money would follow. Revenue could not be the goal.

Still, the reality stared her in the face: the investment was wasted. Apart from the money from the FirstChoice purchase, hardly anything else came in. She lost everything and she was back at square one.

However, there were two positives that would be game changers that Gwyneth picked out of the experience.The first was that Faustina Adjagar would become an inspiration to her. Gwyneth watched her and saw someone who had been in the hair and beauty business longer than she had. She watched how she remodelled First Choice to stay relevant whenever the industry changed. Faustina always knew which direction the wind was blowing and has continued to rely on innovation to not remain stagnant.

The second thing she learnt was that she needed to up her knowledge. If lack of knowledge could get her into so huge a hole, then she was determined to learn as much as she could. She read anything that would help her. She was a voracious reader, which made it easier. Years later, when she went to CEIBS for her MBA, it was an investment into her business.

She was determined to build the business for the long term. It was something she saw many business owners did not do. Many could only survive – even thrive – for a relatively short time, but when things changed, they would decline. That was not what Gwyneth saw for herself. The business needed to be sustainable. She saw Hair Senta as a global brand even in its humble beginnings. And for that to happen, she needed knowledge.

Her next step would change the trajectory of her life. She quit her job. She quit her job even while her husband, Charles, was trying to coax her to multitask a little longer. Another phase in Gwyneth's life had come to an end. Gwyneth the banker needed to give way to Gwyneth the entrepreneur.

It was 2012, and she felt the business needed more time than she could afford combining her bank duties with selling hairpieces. Aside selling from her car, she also set up tables on her lawn to attract potential customers. Before Easter, she would host hair sales in her house. Many who passed through suggested she got a store. She knew she needed a store.

Gwyneth was sure she would be excellent at whatever she put her mind to. She just needed the courage to take the leap. And while she felt called to make the business a fulltime venture, the extra encouragement from friends played a part.

Her job had been there to make a difference in the early days. She may have lost her initial investment of $20,000, but she still had a salary. And savings. And help from her husband. These were a buffer. When she was leaving the bank, her parting package was enough to give her fresh capital to work on the dream.

Hair Senta was born.

In order to get closer to her target, she got a small store on Lagos Avenue in East Legon. By starting in one of Accra's prime enclaves, Gwyneth was sounding her intentions. She assumed that once she had a beautiful shop up and running, everybody would come in. She was wrong. She was far away from the life she had known growing up in Laterbiokorshie. Once more, her mother was instrumental. She would convince people to at least visit the shop.

From the very beginning, Hair Senta was swimming against the tide. Many women who visited the shop said in no uncertain terms that the hair was expensive. Some who were blunt told her that the hair was inferior. This after wearing the hair and coming to demand their money back.

These words hurt.

The worst, however, was yet to come.

One day, a woman and her companion entered the shop. Though there were other customers there, this woman was spewing negativity, saying as loudly as she could that the hair was expensive. This went on for many minutes before she went out. Gwyneth was concerned that her behaviour would affect other potential buyers' decisions. She was glad the lady had left.

However, seeing how upset Gwyneth was, the customer walked back in to add insult to injury. "Oh, you're angry that I am expressing myself," she retorted. "I said the hair is too expensive. It's not even good quality."

Gwyneth had had enough. She asked the woman to leave her shop. Her parting shot, however, would leave Gwyneth a scar for life: "You call this thing a shop? This square thing is a shop?" Her laughter rings in Gwyneth's ears to this day.

They say things must get worse before they get better. For Gwyneth, it could not possibly sink any lower than this.

Friends from the bank would call and ask how she was doing. "Fine," she would reply. She was not fine. Sometimes, she missed working for a salary. Now, she was the one paying people even before thinking about paying herself. She needed to find motivation. Any time someone said, "The store is too light," she would remind herself of her vision to go global.

Well-meaning friends asked her to add to her product line. They suggested she sold bags as well. And shoes. And dresses. After all, these were all part of the beauty industry and complemented each other. But she would tell herself, "Gwen, remember the blueprint." If one does not have their own vision, others will draw up their vision for them.

She wanted people to know Hair Senta for having the best human hair in the world. Hair Senta could not sell shoes. Before she was aware what the term was, she had formed her brand identity and was ready to live and die by this. She decided to stay the course.

Charles was a source of inspiration and advice. He was insistent that she not run her first shop on credit. For a new business, this was a tough choice, but she stuck by it. She had heard too many stories of people spending all their valuable time chasing debtors, many of whom did not pay what they owed. In their wake, they left broken relationships and a broken business.

Interestingly, the dream to deal in hair began in 2002. It was not until 2008 that she started selling hair, and in 2012, her first shop was opened. Ten years from conception to realisation. Through dogged hard work, Gwyneth birthed four businesses within the next 10 years of operation: Hair

Senta, Correct Hair, Sales Staff Association and Hair Senta International Beauty Show (HIBS).

After the official opening of Hair Senta in 2012, Gwyneth diversified into wholesale. Correct Hair is a wholesale line for budding business owners who cannot travel internationally for their hair extensions. As of 2021, Hair Senta has a wide distribution network in most of the major regions in Ghana as well: Togo, Benin, the USA, the UK and other countries that are being added. Buyers then sell downstream as entrepreneurs in their own right.

In order to empower salon staff across Ghana – mostly women – Gwyneth set up the Salon Staff Association (formerly the Sales Executive Programme). By paying a token fee, salon workers are onboarded as sales executives. Each of them has their own ID number, and any time a customer goes to Hair Senta to buy hair, they get a discount just by quoting the referrer's ID number. That discounted amount goes to the salon staff that made the recommendation as a commission. By recognising the power of a referral, Gwyneth turned it into a mutually beneficial relationship.

The fourth business she started was Hair Senta International Beauty Show (HIBS), in partnership with Phamous Media Group, a multinational award-winning brands and marketing company. This strategic alliance led to the show being a much bigger success than she had anticipated. Together, they brought about 100 companies from the beauty industry together, some from as near and as far as Nigeria, the UK and the US. L'Oréal and other big players in the industry assembled under one roof for a two-day fair on beauty. It was the first of its kind in Ghana.

As the business has expanded, company culture has grown in importance for Gwyneth. She had heard many chief executives and human capital professionals pay lip service to their organisations being a family. She was determined to live it. "My team, we call ourselves partners," she reveals.

It is a culture built on inclusiveness. Everyone's opinion matters. Challenges are discussed freely in a non-judgemental atmosphere. By continuously ingraining the vision of the company, solutions usually come from other staff in line with where the company is going.

"We compete on customer service." This is a mantra that is constantly repeated. According to Gwyneth, they don't compete on price, product, people or place (location). For any of her businesses, the customer experience is what makes the whole difference. It keeps them coming back and inspiring others to join. This is at the heart of Hair Senta's retention and acquisition strategy, occurring simultaneously through customer service.

It was not until she went to business school that she began to think strategically, being intentional about putting the customers' needs first. Keeping her initial experience in mind, Gwyneth was even more determined to learn all she needed to know.

She learnt about the pyramid, knowing how many people were at the top, how many people were middle class, and how many were at the bottom of the pyramid. For someone selling luxury goods, this was valuable information. And yet, at the same time, she learnt from experience that the Ghanaian market does not always conform to such neat stratifications. For example, the expectation is that people with a certain amount of disposable income would be willing to spend on certain things. That was not always the case. Ability to pay does not always translate into willingness to pay. Targeting only the affluent was thus not a sustainable business model for the long term. In 2015, when the targeting model changed, Hair Senta became profitable almost overnight.

And yet, for all their success and innovation, Gwyneth insists that their most important value is integrity. While Hair Senta is in the hair extensions business, their number one product is integrity. It creates loyalty.

Admittedly an overthinker, Gwyneth learnt early on to take lessons from her failures and move on. As she dealt with failure after failure, she discovered that asking questions was a great way to get to the root and to begin unearthing real solutions. She learnt to get closer to the problem to understand it. She learnt to never assume. She learnt that tough seasons and cycles would come.

With success came a brand-new set of challenges. Going from having employee numbers in the single digits to having 20 and then 60 employees around the world was one of the challenges she faced with expansion. The number one quality she searched for in employees was honesty. It was non-negotiable with the numbers she was dealing with. Her natural intuition was also an asset in putting the right team together around her.

So, what does the future hold for Gwyneth Gyimah Addo? As a lifelong learner, she continues to grow, taking and organising sessions in strategy for start-ups, and having entrepreneurs engage with one another. And who knows? After her MBA, she could be gunning for a PhD as well one day if her ambition to lecture in a university is to come to pass.

Until then, Gwyneth continues the path to going global. She taught herself social media marketing, selling mostly through Instagram rather than through traditional channels. Her efforts bore fruit in October 2019 when she won and accepted the sales and marketing prize at the 40 Under 40 Awards in Ghana.

Hair Senta is a homegrown success story. What started as a passion became a hobby, a side business, and now a leading brand with reach all over Ghana and spreading out luxuriantly into the world.

The Hair Senta business model has indeed inspired many young men and women in their business walk and continues to be used for business case studies, these and many other projects by most university and post- graduate students.

If Gwyneth ever doubted the resilience of the baby she built, the coronavirus pandemic of 2020 showed her that she was doing something right. The changes in the world brought tremendous new growth opportunities and accelerated plans which were hitherto progressing at a much slower pace. While competitors within and outside Ghana suffered, she transitioned her business into the digital world while they worked from home, starting with a call centre and an online store. They called this new line Last Call Deals. These continue to be part of the business model today.

During the lockdown, she also branched into a new area, becoming a full-time business strategist and training over 100 entrepreneurs in one-on-one sessions via Zoom. Between 2020 and 2021, over 500 entrepreneurs have benefited from her modules to rave reviews.

In July 2021, the Leading Senta was also established, grooming budding young leaders through a series of business strategy sessions.

Finally, GhanaWigmakers is the latest in the family, employing salon owners in rural areas to become part of the value chain for Ghana's wig-making factory. The objective is to supply the world market and reduce the level of imports, while growing Ghanaian exports through the business. In the long run, it provides new employment streams in the industry.

Like most entrepreneurs and high-flying executives, there has been a price to pay. There have been times Gwyneth has been working on some digital marketing when her children complained that she preferred being on her phone to being with them. In times like this, she takes inspiration from former PepsiCo CEO, Indra Nooyi, who intimated that successful woman cannot have it all, because success like that is impossible without some painful trade-offs and sacrifices.

After a decade in business with more ups than downs (though the beginning was full of downs), Gwyneth feels equipped to share some advice for up-and-coming entrepreneurs from her own experience: do not start with assumptions, do your research, have a mentor, be willing to absorb criticism, have faith in God.

On that last point, Gwyneth is sure that Hair Senta has been a miracle. The good breaks have gone her way. As an uncertain beginner, she dreamt of taking her business to the world. Today, she receives orders from the UK and the US. While the raw material is not Ghanaian, people have found her to be a trustworthy partner to do business with.

In her own words, "God has been my guiding principle, He's equipped me with wisdom and has always given me direction, and every single day, I have a fresh burst of ideas and I don't even know where they come from. All I can say is that God has something to do with it."

In 2023, Hair Senta's new worldwide headquarters will open in Accra. The land has been acquired and construction is ongoing. By then, the global hair extensions industry is bound to be worth around $10 billion. Gwyneth Gyimah Addo and Hair Senta are determined to scoop a share of that from right here in Ghana.

Gwyneth's favourite quote, acquired from her father, reads, "Youth is a blessed time, but the blessedness of youth is only and fully realised when it has passed." Therefore, Gwen ensures each day counts as it is considered a blessed opportunity.

From a failed $20,000 investment to a global business. Not bad for a girl under 40 who dared to dream an impossible dream.

CASE STUDY FOUR

KWASI APPIAGYEI

CHAPTER 5

STICK WITH THE CAUSE: NO RETREAT, NO SURRENDER.

KWASI APPIAGYEI

Success is not final; failure is not fatal: it is the courage to continue that counts.

Winston Churchill

When Kwasi Appiagyei opened his acceptance letters to Clarion University and Edinboro University, both in Pennsylvania, he could already see himself adapting to the American way of life. That both came with full scholarship offers only served as icing on the cake. His hard work had paid off and he would be joining his two older brothers across the Atlantic Ocean in North America, ready to build the future he had envisioned for himself.

And then, heartbreak.

After months of applications to schools and to the Embassy of the United States of America, after nurturing dreams and making plans, his father broke the news to him bluntly,

"You're going to stay here with me and be my apprentice."

The same man who gave all his bank statements to support the process was watching Kwasi's admission and five-year student visa go to waste. Instead, father and son found themselves in the water business in the early 2000s struggling to survive in an industry that was nothing like it is today.

To those who know him, however, this was just another opportunity for Kwasi to shine. If there was one word that defined him at that point – and continues to do so today – it would be "consistency".

Born in Amakom, Kumasi, on 23rd March 1980, Kwasi and his family would eventually move to Accra while he was still in primary school. At Modern International School in the Amakom area to State Experimental School in Danyame, in the heart of Kumasi, Kwasi showed an aptitude for learning. Their relocation when he was in Class Four brought the first shock of Kwasi's young life that would force him to map out strategies for survival in a competitive world.

Achimota Primary School. Itwas a totally different experience from what he was used to. From being peerless at the top of the class in Kumasi, he slipped to 33rd out of 35 students after his first term at Achimota Primary.

Among his classmates were President Jerry John Rawlings' daughter and current Member of Parliament for the Klottey

Korle Constituency in Accra, Honourable Zanetor Agyeman-Rawlings, present Deputy Minister of Finance and Member of Parliament for the Atiwa East Consistuency in the Eastern Region, Honourable Abena Osei Asare, and a son of Fred Ohene-Kena, a political stalwart of the 1990s. It was not uncommon to have military bodyguards there with them on campus, not only because of the president's daughter but because it was a school for the leading figures of the Provisional National Defence Council (PNDC) and later the National Democratic Congress (NDC), both ruling entities of Ghana at the time.

Kwasi's failure after his first exams was enough to break him. His sterling performances in Kumasi were enough to get him admission into Achimota Primary without having to write an entrance exam. And yet, here he was, exposed and embarrassed.

But Kwasi does not know how to break. His ambition was shaped, and he took his learning seriously. By the end of Class Six and on the cusp of entering Junior Secondary School, Kwasi was a changed boy. He averaged a position of fifth or sixth.

He had his own personal challenges to overcome. While he had a knack for numbers, and easily grasped mathematical concepts suited for that age – he felt comfortable always attempting new ways to solve the same mathematical problem – English was a different hurdle. Perhaps it had to do with coming from an environment where Twi was more widely spoken, even in school.

Whatever the cause, Kwasi would embark on an intentional journey to improve his English. After all, when his father could honestly say that his son spoke English as if he was speaking in tongues, it was clear that something needed to be done.

Mistake after mistake did not deter him. He would repeat the things he wanted to say until he got them. Deep within, he had a steely resolve to not be held back by his inability to communicate. Friends who had come from Kumasi as well to Achimota Primary begged their parents to transfer them to other schools. For Kwasi, however, this was the fire that was forging his consistency.

The next step in his educational journey took him to Labone Secondary School in Accra, where Kwasi flashed leadership potential and learned to build on it. In those days, prefects were not voted into power as part of a democratic process. Rather, they were handpicked among the lot. This gave Kwasi the opportunity to build upon everything he had learnt as a house prefect in Achimota Primary. Teachers would be comfortable delegating responsibilities to him while they were away for staff meetings. He learned to convince his fellow students about a course of action they would collectively take. As part of his own personal toolkit, he discovered which leadership style suited him best and allowed him to get the results he was looking for.

Unfortunately, this was the end of the road for Kwasi where formal schooling was concerned. His father's plans were to give him a baptism of fire into the world of business, enough to toughen him up and prepare for the rigours of entrepreneurship.

Kwasi's father was a strong believer in apprenticeship. To him, the hands-on approach was the greatest teacher. Why he chose that path for Kwasi and not for his two older brothers remains a mystery. Perhaps he saw something in him that he had not seen in the two before him. Maybe having named Kwasi after himself, he felt he needed to pour his essence into him. Who knows?

Either way, that was how Kwasi Appiagyei would become his father's right-hand man while his friends went to the universities and polytechnics. (A few years later when online classes became more mainstream, Kwasi took informal courses at Pennsylvania State University rather than a full degree course.)

Instead, he sent his son on trips to manufacturing factories around the world to observe and implement on his return. His short stints abroad – never more than three months – taught him so much about manufacturing in the developed world. He visited factories in Germany, Sweden, Hong Kong, and China.

By the age of 22, perhaps just about the same time, his mates would be graduating from their chosen tertiary institutions. He had all the information he needed to make a career in manufacturing. Or did he?

In the late 1990s, the bottled water industry had begun to blossom in Ghana. That was when Kwasi's father started his water brand, Yes Mineral Water, in Kumasi. There was one major stumbling block, though: the location of the factory was far away from the distribution and market sources.

As quickly as this challenger brand emerged, it fizzled out. The distance starved the life out of their operations, and in the year 2000, the business was teetering on the brink of collapse.

For the first time in his young life, Kwasi asked himself what his purpose was. In those introspective moments, watching the factory's output diminish, watching them bleed revenue, watching the staff leave and feeling powerless to do anything about it, Kwasi felt old and desperate. This felt like the end of his life.

However, anybody who has spent just an hour with him would attest to his perseverance. Having started as the factory director, he got a front row seat to the demise. It was like watching a shooting star's glory fade in the night sky. Still, the bombshell was yet to come.

One day, Kwasi's father informed him that the business was folding, and he was moving back to Accra to start over. The young man could not just let it go. Only 22, he was willing to ride it out on his own without his father.

The factory was about 50 kilometres away from their home at Ahodwo in the heart of Kumasi. As the company's finances dwindled, Kwasi moved into the factory to save himself the trotro ride back home. He went home only over the weekends. As a staunch member of the Seventh Day Adventists (SDA) Church, he did not work on Saturdays, so spent the time at church while the factory was closed to everyone.

Call it the bravado of a young buck, or the foolishness of an inexperienced businessman who does not know when it is time to quit. Whatever it was, the only person who could not really appreciate how dire the situation had got was Kwasi Appiagyei. There was a desire in him to hit back at life. It was internal energy that propelled him to swim against the tide and all the things that he perceived had gone against him. When he had nobody to turn to for support or advice, he looked within.

This was where he realised his policy of consistency.

"There was some fear deep within that I was going to grow old like this," he remembered, "and I think that gave me lots of sleepless nights, enough to make me take very strong decisions."

At that young age, with serious factors against him, nobody would have blamed Kwasi for quitting. In fact, having lived through such a rough time, he does not blame entrepreneurs who fold up when they have done all that they can to save their enterprises.

Kwasi looks back at events in his life that prepared him for this moment. As the youngest of a trio of boys, he got most of the chores dumped on him at home. Hard work, as a result, came to him easily.

Growing up, Kwasi also loved to debate. Or argue. That really depends on who was telling the story of his boyhood. His mother, aunties, and cousins all attest to this love for verbal engagement. He would not stop until he had put his points across. His aim was to convince anyone he argued with. He was vocal. He was calculative. He would only really speak when he saw that he was informed enough to influence his opponent with his position. It was all constructive and positive, but even as one who held strong opinions, Kwasi was at the same time ready to learn. One would not be wrong to call him stubborn, because when he felt he was right, he was immovable.

It was this stubborn streak that guided him through some of his darkest moments when he was down to only one employee whom he had not paid for three months. The two of them manned the whole factory by themselves.

Yet, the decline was steady. From production of 5,000 cases of water a day, they now produced between 20 and 50. This was not justification enough for Kwasi Appiagyei to shut down. He was prepared to go to the bitter end where they could not produce even one. He had a point to prove to himself, to his father who had abandoned the business, and to the world.

In his words, "I had this belief that if I can consistently knock a brick wall with my hand for two years uninterrupted, I can bring it down."

Kwasi's father was now in Accra, trading in Okaishie, a hive of constant activity. He had given up on his investment in the water business but was always only a phone call away from his youngest son. However, as time went on and they lived their separate lives, the former master and apprentice spoke less and less, from once a week until the communication dried up to about once a month. Kwasi could have moved to join his father in the hustle and bustle of Okaishie, but he was committed to the water business now.

In his lonesome moments, he had a lot of time to think about his relationship with his father. He had never really thought his father loved his brothers more than he loved him as the last born, but that seed was now sown in his mind. He realised that he bore deep resentment for him, and it had nothing to do with deserting the water business. Over a large chunk of Kwasi's adult life, he realised that his father's preventing him from going to America was a wound that had not healed. The words still rang in his ears: "I am your father. You're not going anywhere."

Kwasi looked back at himself then, a 17-year-old boy who had not travelled anywhere in life before. He had long dreamed of relocating, and though he had turned this negative into zeal to survive a difficult situation, old hurts die hard.

He blamed his father. He blamed himself. He blamed life. Kwasi was conflicted as his emotions swung like a pendulum. In those days as he sat in the doldrums of failure, he would mutter to himself words that in his heart were directed at his father, "I should have gone. If I had gone, this thing wouldn't have collapsed. You should have just forgotten about me and hired a better person so that things would have gone well with your company."

Still, the persistence that had brought him to this point and kept him from giving up made him see the situation in a different way altogether whenever the clouds of despair passed.

As the years rolled on, he learned to forgive his father and today calls him the best father he could have had. He appreciates his father's having a long-term view of things, and when Kwasi would have been content to come back home on vacations decked in boots and bandanas to show off his good life in America, he did not want him to waste his youth.

His father saw his son fixated on materialism. It did not help that these were the times when email was getting popular. His friends would send pictures from the United States where they were having fun and would come to Ghana at Christmas to show off. Kwasi at a point in his life longed for this, and he despised his father for robbing him of that opportunity.

Would Kwasi have been the man he is today, though, without the treatment his father meted out to him in those early 2000s? Unlikely. The factory experience matured him in ways he had no idea about at the time. He learned so many skills that could only be acquired on the job.

When they could not afford to pay technicians to fix his machines, he learned to do the fixing himself. From changing bulbs to replacing fuses, Kwasi had to get his hands dirty and do what he had to do. He learned plumbing. He learned electricals and engineering. There was no other option. Where would these funds come from to pay for these services?

Eventually, he found a Nigerian supplier who would get him spare parts from Lagos. He went to the internet café at the Kumasi Post Office to research on parts for his machines.

Little did he know at the time that in his desperation, he was about to emerge from the dark tunnel and find the solution that would breathe life into his business and transform the story that would be written about him.

A quote attributed to American novelist Tess Gerritsen goes, "We never know until the beast of opportunity is staring us in the face." This was Kwasi's reality at this moment. Every day, he would search for manufacturers of spare parts that he needed for his machines and write them letters. It took two weeks for letters to get to China or Korea or Germany, and two weeks for them to write back. He wanted to know how much the parts he wanted cost, since it was not uncommon for his suppliers to run out of stock when he needed some.

To his shock, the manufacturers replied that parts that he would buy for the cedi equivalent of $20 in Kumasi would cost about $3 if he bought them directly. Kwasi found that hard to believe, but he thought to himself that this was a chance to raise some badly needed capital for his water business.

That was how he opened a second income stream. By this point, four or five years at the helm, the company revenue was only about the equivalent of $20 a month. He had nothing to lose. He sold his water-production machine to serve as seed capital to acquire the parts that he wanted.

Next, he went to the only bank in the area, Bosomtwe Rural Bank, to open a bank account and deposit the money there.

Telling them about what he wanted to do, the manager agreed to facilitate a loan for him. The only thing missing was collateral.

"My collateral is me," Kwasi told the bank manager.

To everyone else, that sounded like a joke. To Kwasi, his belief in himself was so strong that he meant it. He was taking a bet on himself. He told the bank manager about how he alone with his small factory could buy 10 or more of a part. He calculated the profit margins right there in the office, but it was not enough. This was perhaps the first time Kwasi experienced heartbreak in his life. Why did nobody believe him? Family and friends were of no help. He heard more excuses than he could bear.

He felt led to approach the father of an old friend back in the village. Mr Arthur, at the time a total stranger, was a headmaster in a government school. He all but begged the man to take a chance on him. That was how Mr Arthur led Kwasi back to the bank, agreeing to use his salary as collateral for Kwasi to borrow $1,000 to buy his parts from Asia. He recognised the risk. Mr Arthur recognised the risk. However, Kwasi was so sure that he would succeed. There was no business plan, no marketing strategy, no financial projections. It was raw belief.

Kwasi knew nothing about the world of international freight. He sent the money to the Chinese and set up what is called a grouping shipment, meaning that he joined his merchandise with other individuals who were also importing in bulk. When the items arrived as one at the Tema Harbour, they would be sorted in Accra, with his order being transported to Kumasi. All went well.

A few weeks later, Kwasi received the inventory. He had so many parts cheaply acquired and now needed to move them. He went back to his own suppliers and showed them samples. When he mentioned his offer price, though, they wanted assurance that these were genuine parts. Some asked him if he had acquired them through robbery. "My uncle sent them to me and he's in need of money, that's why," Kwasi replied.

That was how Kwasi Appiagyei disposed of his first shipment for a total of about $8,500, selling to his suppliers – who were now his customers – for about 70% of the price they normally got them for.

He quickly went back to Mr Arthur, his benefactor, to offset the loan and gave him a share of the profits. That was how Kwasi breathed life back into his collapsed factory.

Other entrepreneurs would have concentrated on the huge margins received from the importation and sale of these spare parts, but Kwasi was too invested mentally into the water business. For him, this second stream of income was merely a temporary measure to get the wheels of production running again in his enterprise.

Serendipity:

Many a business has started by accident. This was Kwasi's story. In trying to get his parts more quickly, he became a supplier. The membranes in his factory's water-filtration systems could get damaged and he would be at the mercy of spare-parts dealers. Production would halt for a week while he waited for his suppliers to get some from Germany through Alitalia or KLM. He found a gap in the industry and exploited it for his benefit.

Through his profits, he got the idea to invest in other water businesses. He also relocated his factory to be closer to the business source, plugging a major leak for the business.

Having spent years educating himself on the technical side because he was unable to pay professionals, Kwasi started to modify parts that he imported and took them to the machinists at Suame Magazine to fit them. Over time, he was able to design parts with his Chinese partners so that when these parts arrived, they were ready for use.

Despite the success of this side operation, he remained consistent. Everything led to a reinvestment in the water business. Consistency.

It was all about Plan A. Somewhere in his formative years, Kwasi had heard a speaker talk about people who had a fallback plan not being likely to work hard on their main plan. True or not, Kwasi imbibed it. He put all his eggs in one basket and fought for it.

To him, that is why the tales of entrepreneurial journeys are littered with school dropouts finding success. They had no other options, and they have a chip on their shoulder. The energy is different. Without a formal university education, Kwasi put himself in the same category.

Today, he thinks about how he could have left the factory behind and got a job. He thought about the negative voices that would have told him that he had collapsed his father's business. In his mind, that would not be his defining story. He was determined to make a name for himself in the water business, even if it meant refining seawater. The core was always water, and he remains unready to deviate from that, even though he has been presented with opportunities in mining, real estate, and more.

"There is no Plan B," Kwasi reminds himself resolutely. In the world of water, it was sink or swim. He was all in.

So long as it has to do with water, Kwasi is interested. Now, he has about eight shops around Ghana. He provides water solutions from A to Z. From domestic supply to the dozens of branches in industrial services, his fingerprints are all over the industry. Not only will he drill boreholes for homes and industries, for example, but he will test its suitability for internal and external use. He has water filtration shops in Accra, Kumasi, Takoradi, Koforidua, Sunyani and more.

Today, Kwasi provides water services for food manufacturers and multinationals including Nestlé, KFC and Papaye Foods for them to have quality water. He also supplies local pharmaceutical giants like Kinapharma and Ernest Chemists for their syrups and herbal medications.

In all this expansion, Kwasi still produces water in eight production plants.

What happened to the side business that served as the catalyst for getting Kwasi back on his feet? He continues to supply over 400 water producers with manufacturing machines, replacements parts, consumables and more to ensure that their production is never negatively impacted.

Nearly two decades on, he continues to marvel about how both arms of the business gave rise to each other. The equipment branch was birthed from the manufacturing branch, but without manufacturing, equipment would never have been conceived.

From those uncertain days where he had a single employee, he now runs an operation with over 400 staff on payroll.

Almost 70% of them are women. To Kwasi, he has a responsibility to build the value chain, because the benefits trickle down to the community level and to families. Those downstream find new ways to better their lot, growing the industry from the grassroots to the top, and creating an ecosystem where the big players and start-up entrepreneurs all profit.

Kwasi strongly believes that everything that we are blessed with, from money to knowledge to influence, are all for the benefit of others. In dividing his business into buildings, machinery, and people, only people can never be bought. He has had to kneel to apologise to and beg a resigning employee to stay because of the value they brought to the business.

This investment in his people is a core part of his leadership style. That is why there have been staff who have been with him for about 15 years. That is why some have resigned only to return after a while. Even people who were let go for bad behaviour have been allowed back after proving they have reformed, though with stricter conditions.

Kwasi's love for sharing knowledge is reflected here in giving others the opportunity to grow in their own space and in their own direction. "The best way to let people grow is to share with them," he says philosophically.

Knowledge. Not money. And that is why he gives his employees a seat at the management table, from the lowest to the highest. His knack for debate continues all these years later. Every section of the business has a representative. Where somebody does not make contributions for several sittings, they are duly replaced. Also, where another just rubber stamps the opinions of the majority, they too have not understood the role of dissenting views in the overall growth of the business and are made to give way to others. These are tried and tested principles that have resulted in growth in the business.

That means that at weekly management meetings, the leadership comes with the expectation to be drilled by the mid-level managers and other representatives as a means of maintaining self-health. It is better to hear criticism internally than from the customer.

The culture of innovation remains unabated. New ideas continue to grow and benefit the business. For example, together with his Chinese partners, he was able to repurpose perfume diffusers to dispense chlorine in safe quantities, which became invaluable during the COVID-19 pandemic. These have continuously been modified to become rechargeable and to spray at different angles. It is this kind of innovation that creates jobs down the line. Ultimately, everyone benefits.

From his initial attempts to get funding, however, Kwasi learnt that nobody would believe in his dream like he did. After presenting his ideas for his chlorine diffuser to four of his bankers, (some of whom he had been with for over a decade) for two hours each in October 2020, he was met with rejections and excuses. Some believed the market was not ready. He was seeking a partnership with these banks for his company, Adair Ghana, and not just a loan. He assured them that they would end up being his customers instead if he got help elsewhere. After the success of the product, true to his prediction, one of these banks bought over 100 of the diffusers for their branches.

"The bank is never your friend until you are a rich man," he says wistfully. "The bank will give you a million when you have millions in assets, so technically you have what you need from them already. No bank will give you more than what you don't have in terms of assets and other things." This is a life lesson he learned over two decades of doing business in Ghana.

Along the way, he has also learned from disappointments as a normal part of business. Whether it is huge unbudgeted expenses or being shocked by the behaviour of once-trusted staff, there have been blows that he has had to take on the chin and move on. Embezzlement, disregard for authority and worse have rocked him, but he remains standing.

The story of Kwasi has been one of how consistency has seen him from the depths of failure to the heights he has now reached. And consistency in his purpose will take him further to areas he can only dream about.

His belief in God is unshakable. Too many bounces have gone his way for him to believe it is about his own smarts and influence. He says, "I belong to the school of practical religion that tells you that you can do all things through Christ who strengthens us and the same one that says that a man must work hard too."

He saw his father shut his Okaishie shop on Saturdays, the busiest days in the market, to observe the Sabbath, and still come out richer than others who were open seven days a week.

He still gives his first fruits to the church, even drilling a borehole for the church before drilling one for himself. He donated the first chlorine diffusers to not only his local SDA church, but also to the International Central Gospel Church (ICGC) and Church of Pentecost in the Achimota area.

"In the end, I want to be like Christ," Kwasi concludes. "I am envious of Him because of the way He is. I want to be like my Heavenly Father."

From the heartbreak of having to give up his scholarships and university admission to failure in the water business to finding his own way, with Adair, Kwasi Appiagyei has been through the ringer. However, if water always finds its level, the man who has dedicated his life to water will also find new areas to leave his mark.

CASE STUDY FIVE

KOFI ANKU

CHAPTER 6

FINDING HOME ON A BRIDGE

KOFI ANKU

"There's nothing more beautiful than someone who goes out of their way to make life beautiful for others."

Mandy Hale

In 2021, Google completed an acquisition for fitness brand Fitbit for a sum of over $2 billion. The news brought a smile to Kofi Anku's face when he heard.

When you can count among your schoolmates a founder of Fitbit, it is easy to feel awed. After all, not everyone can claim to be on a first-name basis with an innovator whose startup has taken the world by storm. The truth is, success was expected of the students of this private boys' high school, with many of them ending up in Ivy League colleges. For them, it was not a question of whether you would achieve greatness, but in what field. From those performing in Broadway musicals right after graduation to classically trained concert pianists, these accomplishments were not out of the ordinary.

For Kofi Anku, being in the midst of such brilliant minds was only a step to the fast-paced journey of high achievement. For him, however, he cut his teeth at home.

Though born to Ghanaian parents, his upbringing had more than a sprinkling of international flavour. One could say that the genetic lottery was kind to him when it came to academic ability and entrepreneurial fortitude.

Speaking of his family and upbringing Kofi said, "My mother was born in the UK and my father born in Alavanyo. He came to the States after graduating from Mawuli Secondary School in Ho. And then, he won a full scholarship to his school in Iowa and went on to become a Cancer Specialist. My parents, my brother and sister were part of a very comfortable middle-class community in Ohio."

As the youngest child, a lot of leadership roles fell to his brother who was five years older. Still, there were leadership positions that Kofi was able to take up at school, especially in high school.

In the Anku household, however, while academics were high priority – Kofi's brother was always academically gifted throughout their school years – they were enrolled in competitive sports from an early age. This was a normal part of American education. From the age of five, Kofi was already partaking in swimming competitions. This emphasis on youth sports would see him try his hands at American football and more. Unknown to him, this was developing in him a steely determination to win at all costs and the temperament to overcome setbacks. These characteristics would serve him well in the years to come.

Comparing sports to business, he said, "I think Americans see sports as a metaphor for business and in many ways, there are lots of parallels."

To Kofi, these are advantages that he brings into Ayi Mensah Park and other businesses he runs in Ghana. He sees the dedication needed in the world of sports to shave a few seconds off swim times or to lose an amount of weight for optimal performance as being the same will that is needed to reach one's targets in the world of business.

As part of his American education, programmes and organisations were as integral to the curriculum as algebra and history. It was on the field of play and in club meetings that soft skills were picked up: negotiating different social landscapes, motivating the team on a rainy day at training, rallying the troops.

Kofi said, "I think largely, the education system we inherited is part of a colonial legacy, so Ghanaians typically – and you can see this often – are very well educated but often we are not creative."

While Kofi could hold his own in the classroom, he did not top the class, and that was fine by him. He realised early that his passions lay elsewhere, and he gave himself a wide range to explore these. That's what led him to spend a semester in Amman, the capital of Jordan, while in school. Through a Korean=American family, he learnt to speak Korean when he started going to their Korean church.

The best thing of all was that his parents not only allowed it, but they actively encouraged them to discover things for themselves wherever life led.

Dr & Mrs Anku taught their children that life involved risk. Especially entrepreneurship. So, while Ghanaians could find themselves easily as civil servants or even occupying top roles in the United Nations as lawyers and consultants, we are collectively lovers of risk. This was one cultural difference Kofi saw from his everyday existence in America. While he sees entrepreneurship in our personalities, it is lacking in our educational system.

Kofi learnt about the value of things at an early age. He ventured into his first entrepreneurial activity before the age of 12, engaging in the long-held pastime of trading baseball cards among his friends. This was a whole economy among children, with some of these cards going for hundreds of dollars. Buying cards and selling the most popular ones at a profit excited him. These were his initial steps into a fast-paced life in the future far away from suburban Ohio.

While the seed was planted in the playgrounds and alleys of his school and community, it was nurtured by knowledge he picked up as he matured; specifically, the struggle of African-American citizens of the United States of America. Though born years after the height of the civil rights movement, Kofi was witness to how Black people in America did not have the same opportunities based on a factor they had no control over: skin colour.

He noted that "people of African descent have been treated as second-class citizens for a huge part of American history. So, the idea of having our own country where Africans could enjoy first-class citizenship becomes more meaningful when you have built businesses and institutions where you can enjoy the same quality of life that you would enjoy in the west here at home."

This was a huge driver for him. It was the best of both worlds. As a Ghanaian citizen with an American education, he could build the life he wanted for himself with the tools and knowledge he had picked up working in the largest economy in the world.

An Ivy League education opens doors. While studying African American Literature and History for his bachelor's degree in Columbia University in New York City, Kofi picked up the hard skills he needed to run a business. He saw parallels between the Pan-African independence struggle and the

African American civil rights movement. Colonialism and the founding of nations aligned with leaders in the Black community rallying the people to a higher purpose.

The first presidents of Ghana and Nigeria, Drs Kwame Nkrumah and Nnamdi Azikiwe respectively, developed their oratory skills in Black churches while attending Historically Black Colleges and Universities (HBCUs) in America. The fertile grounds for a push for change even attracted Malcolm X and Maya Angelou to visit Ghana.

Beyond political emancipation, they sought economic freedom. These were themes that resonated well with Kofi.

As one who had a total immersive experience in the American educational system, Kofi credits a lot of his business success to the confidence instilled in him throughout his formative years. From seeing some of the world's most influential people in the halls of his school to the constant reminders the students received that they could do anything they put their minds to, Kofi really bought into message that the world is your oyster, and you can do anything you really want to do.

From an early age, he was taught to enter a room and ask for what he needs from anyone in a position to help. At the same time, this confidence made potential partners comfortable enough to do business. That was what it was all about.

A big part of Kofi's entrepreneurial journey that cannot be overlooked belongs to his parents. In fact, the very beginnings of his real estate ambitions started by observing the impressive real estate portfolio that his father built up alongside excelling in his private medical practice.

Speaking of his inspiration, he said, "My father was one of 14 children of his parents, and he has an incredible amount of discipline and focus on his career."

He picked up his father's extraordinary work ethic and his appetite for risk. And as his mother complimented his father, they were the perfect tag team to achieve the things they dreamed of. This they did by investing heavily in properties in Florida. Both parents were intentional about teaching their children the rudiments of the trade. They spent a lot of time around these properties when Kofi was still a boy.

"I think a lot of times," Kofi remarked, "it's important just having that kind of exposure at a young age and seeing it is possible to own these investments and bear the responsibility for them."

These were the roots of Kofi's desire to be a producer rather than a consumer, and they would shape him in all his business pursuits.

The flagship of his entrepreneurial endeavours, Ayi Mensah Park, is a product of all the lessons Kofi picked up at the dinner table, while talking to his father, in the hallways at school,in the neighbourhood streets, and in life in general. He learnt the lesson of failing fast.

"How many businesses have I started?" Kofi asks himself. "I don't know," he responds. Always happy to try out a new idea, it is not uncommon to see him put a bit of money into a small venture and see what it yields. After all, there is always a positive to get from even businesses that fail. From key relationships to important lessons, there is always something to pick up in every business. Kofi sees businesses as a seed to be planted. For some, the business was revived later with the right partner or the right factors in play.

As a serial entrepreneur and a lifelong student, it is not strange to hear Kofi say that he has learnt more from failed businesses than he has lost. It starts with not taking the failure personally and knowing that this is no indication that he will not make it tomorrow.

Kofi says, "It just means that that particular venture didn't work. I keep enough distance from it to be able to examine it. Why did it not work? Did I take the wrong approach? Did I bring on the wrong partners? Did we not have the right resources? Was it the wrong opportunity?"

Interestingly, this is the same approach he has taken to businesses that have been successful. It is this clinical view that ensures he is not emotionally invested in the failure or the success so much that it becomes damaging.

When it comes to business, however, Kofi is not one to hog the spotlight and take all the glory. At the same time, he knows that success is not in how big the team is, but how they work together to achieve their desired outcomes.

It all begins with partnership.

"I actually think it is easier to keep a very lean team and to find people who have aligned visions to collaborate with. What I found most successful for me is to multiply my impact in the world by partnering with people that share similar visions. So, it's not really a question of me trying to impart an idea that I have in my mind into a number of other people but finding people who want to be on my team who already have a similar set of values and a similar goal."

Despite a knack for entrepreneurship both by nature and by nurture – he also owns a greenhouse business to grow vegetables year-round – real estate is Kofi's primary business. Whether it is actual development like with Ayi Mensah Park or dealing with undeveloped plots of land, Kofi understands the real estate business in Ghana.

On one hand is creating the product and marketing it. This comes with big risk. For instance, getting the group of contractors together to bring a dream into reality comes with its own attendant risks at every stage of the development. It should appeal to his target in Ghana and in the United States.

On the other hand, there is the land business. Anybody who has attempted to acquire land in Ghana knows that it is not the most straight-forward process. Neither is it the cleanest. From land being sold multiple times to failed promises, the land acquisition process is littered with story after story of woe. That is where Kofi comes in with aggregating plots of land together, making sure that the paperwork is in place, cleaning up the title, getting permits for access roads, and then selling of individual plots to people who want to avoid the headache of buying from the traditional chiefs.

This business model did not come about by accident. By putting himself in the place of the frustrated customer, Kofi simply had to ask himself what he wanted and solve the problem. As anyone would know, though, this is easier said than done.

It was not hard to come up with the concept for Ayi Mensah Park. Being typically upper-middle class himself, Kofi asked himself what amenities he was looking for in a neighbourhood where he felt his children could play basketball and go for a swim. By recognising his pain points and working to fix them, he had a fair idea of what would resonate with buyers like him. And who would not want their children to have the freedom to run and play in a two-acre park for the community?

Kofi is not shy to say that Ayi Mensah Park was designed to run like an American neighbourhood. That was what he knew. The perspectives he picked growing up in a foreign culture made it easy to present something new on the market to his target. To him, storing water in tanks and having a septic tank on the property constituted cultural shock. How about building a community where the homeowner did not have to think about these? How about the property developer dealing with water and sewerage at the community level? That added efficiency not only gave the owners less to think about, but it brought the costs down. What was there not to like about that?

And while thinking about radical ideas for prospective buyers, some of the homes in Ayi Mensah Park generated their own energy, so they were completely off-grid. While not handled at the community level like water and sewerage, this appealed to a select clientele.

For a dream that was probably 15 years in the making, Kofi and his team had to get it right. When he first moved back to Ghana, his family had a handful of properties that they had acquired over the years. But then, Kofi's vision was much bigger. For the scale that he was dreaming of, they had the challenge of getting the resources and partnerships to transition from conceptualising to actualising.

This is where Black Ivy comes in.

Led by Cheryl Mills, an African-American investor, Black Ivy is a project developer based in the United States that was looking for collaborations on the African continent. Through his dealings in the real estate space in Ghana, Kofi and Cheryl were introduced to each other by several mutual contacts on both sides of the Atlantic.

Speaking of the breakthrough, Kofi revealed, "It turned out not only were they interested in residential real estate, but we also had a similar vision, and they could bring resources. They didn't have land here, but they had resources they could bring and required to be developed, so we could collaborate on this development."

As fate would have it, the business plans for Ayi Mensah Park were already in place. A previous collaboration with an investment group in the United Kingdom had fallen through about a year before the Black Ivy partnership. Over time, the plans were refined, including the price points after the various architects, contractors and engineers brought their costs. The plans were signed on. There was no turning back.

In the end, Ayi Mensah Park yielded $30 million in sales.

To say that Ayi Mensah Park is the jewel in the crown for Kofi would be stating the obvious. It was the culmination of hard work in a tough industry. Before that, Kofi and his team did what they had to do to survive. Their priority was stretching their capital while biding their time.

Referring to the low points in the business cycle, Kofi said, "Before we even started this project, we were involved in land sales and other developing projects. We really had to keep an eye on our cash flow and kept a very lean team to make sure we were not spending money that our business was going to need, going forward."

At the same time, selling land also served as a buffer. When business was slow, plots they owned in Pokuase could easily be offloaded to make funds available for other development projects.

As a strategy, he has used bank debt sparingly at low debt-to-equity ratios and backed by contractual revenues. He is convinced that going with the banks would have bankrupted his company.

Ultimately, he advises upcoming entrepreneurs to know what form of financing works best for them: "You really need to know whether or not equity is the right thing for you to take on to your business or you look for an equity partner or a debt partner, because if it takes you longer to sell whatever it is you think you are making up your margins at the time you hoped, that could be a problem."

The Ayi Mensah Park experience taught Kofi something, but being a firm believer in process, he does not count it as a regret. The external funds that made the dream possibly took his focus elsewhere. Rather than concentrating on the nuts and bolts of the venture, as most Ghanaian business owners tend to do, Kofi learnt to have a global vision, and for him, the international capital was transformational, not only in his development, but also in his business outlook. Imagine what could have been if he had discovered this earlier.

He continued, "The big story for us in many ways is that real estate is a hugely complex business. You can buy a lot of talent. The challenge really has been attracting the right financing. That has always been the biggest challenge."

Anyone who wants to be in the real estate space needs to have a plan and be ready to play the long game. Otherwise, one might as well import fizzy drinks for short-term gains.

Kofi is the embodiment of "don't put all your eggs in one basket". He caught the entrepreneurship bug early and parlayed it into a lifestyle. While real estate is his pride and joy, an experiment with his mother bore fruit, literally and figuratively.

His mother once sent him tomatoes from London, which he grew in buckets in his house. Another idea was birthed when he saw the potential in growing vegetables. "We have actually had three different interventions or innovations we were working on," Kofi said.

The first was with virtually no money. Just seeing what grew and how the market responded was the bait that he and an American friend used to rope in a larger investment.

Diversifying

The next innovation was at Ayi Mensah Park, this time with an American firm, where they established a large aquaponics development farm and attracted interest. Here too, another recommendation helped to make for an even bigger development to feed into a long-term vision. It is this flexibility that has helped Kofi in business, taking the good with the bad without taking his eye off the prize.

The developer-turned-farmer sees simplicity in the farmers of Ghana. No matter the scale of the farm, the vision is the same: to grow, sell, and put food on the table. For Kofi, that is a very special thing, and a privilege that he does not take lightly at all.

Not one to rest and enjoy his achievements, Kofi is already on to the next thing. This is not to say that he does not appreciate Ayi Mensah Park, but he has learned his lessons for the future, and is incorporating them into his next venture. While there were obstacles, he does not see them as disappointments, but mental notes to consider in the next phase of his personal development.

Indeed, the vision is not to build hundreds of homes. No, it goes beyond that. Kofi dreams of building tens of thousands of homes in his lifetime. This goes back to his relationship with the Korean family. He learnt that in South Korea, their transformation occurred over the span of a few generations. Armed with that knowledge, it fired something up in his belly.

That said, it would be too much of a sanitised report to say that Kofi had discovered the touch of gold with every business he got into. Like all entrepreneurs, he has suffered painful loss in the past. "Failure is an integral part of success. I know enough successful people and know enough about their stories to know what you see in the glossy magazines is not their full lived experience."

Building a legacy that outlives the individual is going to come with setbacks, but nobody got to the top without a few battle scars.

Looking back, he recalled, "One of the businesses that I was dead keen to push forward when I came to Ghana twenty-something years ago was a chocolate brand for the U.S. market. I even had the wrapper designed. I was never able to get that off the ground and now twenty years later, there are quite a few market entrants who are doing really good work in that space. I don't find that massively disappointing. In some ways it confirmed the fact that my instincts were right, that this was something that could be marketed globally successfully."

One lesson Kofi learnt in coping with the ebbs and flows of business is to not get too high on the highs or too low on the lows.

For all his success, Kofi is humble enough to know that he is only as good as the team that is around him. While he has always surrounded himself with a small team of hard workers, the chief traits he looks out for are character and competence, and integrity is foundational to character.

Anybody can acquire hard skills. If he needs an MBA, he hires one. But when it comes to integrity, for instance, all other values grow out of it, and either one has it or one does not have it. He believes that there is nothing that a committed team cannot achieve. Knowing that he has no architectural or engineering training, he has learnt to rely on the technocrats in the room. At the same time, he uses his handicap as an opportunity to ask as many questions as come to mind without allowing ego to get in the way.

That is one of his strengths: seeing connections and bringing people together in collaborative spaces. The satisfaction does not come from being right, but from solving problems together.

For any businessman, the biggest problem may be selling a product. History is littered with great products that sat on shelves without moving. In ensuring that this would not be his lot, Kofi invested in technology to get the story out. Interestingly, these were low-cost technologies. Whether it was YouTube, Facebook or LinkedIn and other non-traditional marketing tools, Kofi took a keen interest in anything that would give him a leg up on the competition and get his product in front of potential buyers and potential partners.

Having reached the customer, the product practically sells itself. Kofi has always insisted on going the extra mile and giving the customer what he would like if he were the one buying, for example, making sure that the cabinets do not need to be redone a year after moving into the home or that the doors close properly. The house must be an experience and being part of the community should leave lingering feelings of positivity for as long as the homeowner lives there.

The challenge now is to ensure that anyone can buy a home. This means being intentional about dropping the price. The aim right now is to get classy two-bedroom homes that cost south of $40,000 from the present prices in the $140,000 range. After dabbling in the world of the upper-middle class, low-cost housing is a challenge Kofi is licking his lips to take on board. As development gets progressively cheaper, Kofi sees the day units go as low as $25,000 and still make a decent profit for the developer.

Thoughts like these are enough to keep any man awake at night. It is not the easiest thing to switch off at the end of the day. Not for Kofi: "Exercise is still a very central part of how I deal with stress, and I am pretty hands-on with my kids. They are far more important than any of the businesses that I have ever been involved with. I think perspective taking is very key. If you just focus on a specific problem in your business, it can become overwhelming but when you can put your business in the perspective of your family – your most important relationships – it allows you to minimise the amount of stress that emanates from a specific kind of problem."

At the heart of everything, however, is purpose.

Kofi keeps himself grounded by asking himself, "Who are you and why are you doing what you are doing?" This is what allows him to remain even keeled in the face of bumps on the road to where he is going. Where a change in course is needed, it is measured against the purpose. Kofi lives by the mantra that there are multiple ways to succeed in business.

Those would be his parting words to any aspiring entrepreneur: find the gap in the market and offer solutions to the world.

Yet, even before that, Kofi believes that the entrepreneur should just start. "What I bristle against is when people look at entrepreneurs and think that there is something they can learn from them when they haven't initiated their entrepreneurial journey themselves."

Many years ago, Kofi Anku started out on his entrepreneurial journey. He has no intention of stopping any time soon.

CASE STUDY SIX

THERESA OPPONG BEEKO

CHAPTER 7

CHALLENGE THE STATUS QUO.

THERESA OPPONG- BEEKO

"Be so good they can't ignore you."

Steve Martin

Failure has a way of bringing out a reaction in people. Some quit straight away. Why risk feeling the dread of helplessness again? Some hang on a little longer and then fade away. Some try again, and some try something else.

And then, there are some like Theresa Oppong-Beeko who are forged through failure.

On the surface, events in her life looked straightforward. From the beginning, her life followed a linear path. Growing up in Tamale throughout her formative years gave her perspectives of life in the north of Ghana. Entering the University of Ghana in 1981 after completing her A-Levels at Tamale Secondary School was a new experience and represented the next stage of her development. Thanks to a year's break when the university closed down, she graduated in 1985 and did her national service at the Department of Sociology for two years. By 1990, she had completed her MBA at the University of Ghana's School of Administration.

However, it was one event wedged between these years that would change Theresa's life forever.

In the late 1980s, Theresa (known to her friends as" Tess") identified the fishing business as one that she could make a mark – and some money – in. The governing Provisional National Defence Council (PNDC) at the time was giving facilities to individuals who were interested in agribusiness. While in her final year, she had made her decision to throw her hat into the ring and applied. The woman who had grown up in dry arid conditions in the North was venturing into unknown waters – into an industry that has been a mainstay of the South from time immemorial.

From the very start, she was on the back foot. Insufficient funds suffocated the young business, and eventually, the banks' inability to support the business suffocated it before it could gather any momentum. In a year, she was as far away from the Tema Fishing Harbour as one could imagine and was back in the classroom.

Experiencing failure in the fishing industry would be a turning point. It resulted in her going all in for her MBA. She discovered that she had to beef up her knowledge in management principles if she was to survive in the cutthroat world of business. While she believed that getting one's hands dirty was the best way to learn, she felt getting a business education would be empowering.

Yes, she knew that her future lay in the world of business despite the initial setback, but the next time she got an opportunity, she would be ready.

Stubborn. Headstrong. These are words many have used to describe Tess Oppong-Beeko, though few would dare say so to her face. The can-do spirit is a buzzword that is perhaps used a bit too liberally in recent times, but before it was the description of choice for every go-getter, she was a living breathing example.

To those who do not know Tess, her quiet disposition could be deceptive. Hers was a steely determination that from an early age, was simmering underneath. Her competitive spirit shone through even while playing with friends. She would do whatever she wanted to do, irrespective of whether everyone else wanted something else. She was so uncompromising that her mother had to intervene, advising her daughter to be a little flexible. Perhaps being the oldest child had a part to play in shaping her unyielding nature. At the same time, her clear leadership abilities allowed her parents to leave many responsibilities in her care. Losing both parents early in her life, unfortunately, forced her to grow up even more, but by the time the unfortunate happened, she was prepared.

While leadership was hoisted on her by virtue of being the firstborn, she still had to learn how to lead in secondary school. As Assistant Girls' Prefect, she kept mostly to herself reading and planning. The strong heroines in her favourite books would inspire her, even though they were mostly Mills & Boon romantic novels she could start and finish in a day. No matter the opposition they faced, they would kiss in the end, and all would be well. She was particularly enamoured by the leading ladies encountering ranch owners and landlords of large estates. The lifestyle intrigued her. And while these fantasies have become real in her life, she still reads them today during her occasional leisure moments.

For many an entrepreneur, the art of selling began during childhood. That was not quite her experience. She had got the entrepreneurial gene from her mother and honed her skills by working in her mother's small shop while on vacation. And yet, even at the age of about 12, she knew she wanted more. She wanted bigger. While staying respectful, she was bold enough to tell her mother – perhaps her first role model – that she was not content with selling small. She had big dreams. She dreamed of buildings.

Tess could not tell you where the desire came from. She had an uncle who was a contractor. On the occasions that she got to visit him, she would go to construction sites with him, though she was not as interested in the civil works as she was in the whole building project. Was that where the seed was planted? She cannot tell.

"For as long as I can remember, I have always loved buildings," she noted, "and even today when I travel, you'll find me looking at buildings coming up, rather than spending time in shops and malls."

Her failure to grow her fishing business may have been notable in her life story, but selling fish was never the dream. It was meant to be a means to an end, a purely financial move. The objective was always and only estates. That is easily explained by the fact that the two businesses she has been involved with in her life to date have been fishing and estate development (diversified into residential properties, commercial properties and a hotel). Perhaps, that was where she discovered two traits that sum up her success as an entrepreneur: endurance and perseverance.

Still, in her quiet moments – which are few and far in between – she has thought about her sojourn into the fishing industry. Could she have achieved more if she had persevered? Could she have been successful if she had shown more endurance? Nobody will ever know.

Years later when the Manet Group was birthed, it was out of this yearning to be who she always wanted to be; the person she was born to be.

Seeking employment was never really on the cards for her. Not even after completing the MBA. She did give it a try, working at the Cocoa Board (COCOBOD) for a year. Deep down, she knew it was not working. She needed to be free. Her father was a lawyer. Her mother owned a shop, a night club and a boutique. Her paternal grandfather was a timber merchant (her father took over the business when she was about 13 years old). Something from deep within her screamed that being a civil servant was out of the question. Her drive just would not allow her to stay seated.

Working in the field she calls her own today taught her so much about herself that she did not know at the time. While she is not one to downplay the positives in formal education, her informal education through experiences, mistakes made, and time spent on projects most likely were major factors in her success. For instance, one cannot learn in a book the things one picks up from meeting different people. While her sociology first degree opened her mind a bit more to the complexities of human interaction, she learnt quickly that the things written in books could be drastically different from real life, based on so many fast-moving variables, from environment to age.

Building a business is hard work. She saw many people crack under the pressure. However, her resilience would just not allow her to quit when the estate development industry threw its worst at her. And for her, part of what it takes to build a robust business is getting people on board who are willing to follow the leader – or who will allow themselves to be dragged along, at least. On this, she is unyielding. "It is like I know where I'm going," she says matter-of-factly, "and I go with those who want to go with me. Those who don't want to go with me, bye."

In her experience, any good entrepreneur is a dictator, and entrepreneurship just does not mix well with democracy. Irrespective of who agrees with her or not, she believes that spending hours debating the way forward results in analysis paralysis.

One decision Tess made which stands out for her was how to differentiate her product offering. Growing up, her family home was in a State Housing Corporation estate. Even as a little girl, she could not stand everyone's house looking like a whole deck of replicas.

On many occasions, visitors got lost with all the houses looking like the one from three streets away. Though she was just a child, an idea began to grow in her. She decided even then that no two houses in her estate would look the same. There would be little differentiators that would add a touch of uniqueness to each home. She may not have known where the passion came from, but knowing it was there and it was strong was enough to push her through hard times. Like a tree growing quietly in an untouched forest, her plans and ideas had been many years in the making, brewing and refining in her mind.

Among other things, she had her business plan in her head. Despite having a graduate degree from business school, she did not mind cutting more than a few corners to get where she wanted to, so long as they remained legal and ethical.

This did not apply to the real business on the ground, though. There were no shortcuts to success. In Ghana in the 1990s, private real estate development was only a fledgling industry. With rapid urbanisation, State Housing Corporation was unable to meet the housing deficit, and the few private companies competing for affordable housing projects created a crowded field.

Over the next two years, she went from inception to implementation of her vision. From negotiating tough land deals to putting up the superstructures, her every waking moment was consumed by her devotion to making her mark in this industry.

Regrettably, many problems from 20 years ago are still problems in Ghana today. Land litigation, limited access to funding and apathy from workers who just do not share in the vision of the project stalled her progress.

Back then, she had to rely on personal finances and loans from friends and family to kick-start the dream. Eventually, she got a lifeline loan facility from NDK Financial Services and UniqueTrust Financial Services. She used other unorthodox means to raise funds, even having barter agreements in place for potential clients. It would probably be a decade of tough guts before she would make a profit.

After all, the interest to pay back was steep, Banks in general around this time were charging interest rates of 48% per annum and Microfinance companies at the time charged double what traditional banks did. Unique Trust, NDK, CDH, etc for example, had rates of 8% per month, translating to almost a mind-blowing 96% per annum. Through these heady days, she learnt not to fear debt. If she did, that would have been the end of her dream.

A lot has changed in the estate development industry over time, however. As of 2021, it is now a burgeoning industry with players of many sizes populating the space. Funding is not as difficult as it was in the 1990s and early 2000s. Still, some things remain the same.

Today, it is not uncommon to find her bartering items to stretch her capital. It was a skill she picked up in her early days which she has not given up yet. When she needs some quick financing, nothing is sacred. To the fainthearted, her selling her own house to complete a project would seem like a step too far. However, for a hard-nosed veteran like Tess who had worked her way up with a touch of the unconventional, everything was on the trading block. The work always came first.

As a personal rule, Tess does not dwell on past regrets. Her focus remained on affordable housing even when newer developers dotted the city with luxury apartments and ritzy new estates. Rather than raise prices, she found ways to squeeze costs. Could she have sold the units for more money? Yes, but her commitment to keeping prices relatively lower would always refocus her. As would be expected, however, it resulted in lower margins and a bit more debt than she had originally intended to carry. Crying over these would just waste time she could spend thinking of solutions, so she just kept moving.

The tight cash flow prevented her from embarking on infrastructural projects in her estates she wishes she could have completed by now. The heavy losses she bore would have made lesser mortals quit. There have been failures she has had to bounce back from. People have let her down and others have put obstacles in the way of realising her plans. Some of these were even done intentionally. She has battle scars that she proudly wears as medals, each failure a story of resilience and bravery.

The Manet Group is profitable today. However, that remains a side note, as money was never at the heart of her business at its humble beginnings. Her desire to build and build more is still an all-consuming one. In her business, she has seen many things that brought her a sense of fulfilment. Despite the opportunities to generate extra revenue she passed on, or the years she endured a balance sheet in the red, she still counts as her greatest achievement, the magic of making something beautiful where there was once nothing.

She still lives for the joy of seeing families move into their brand-new homes. She remembers the land that was cleared for these houses to be built. Where children run around and play today, there once was only bush. Tess recalls, "I remember telling my mother that I am not interested in selling. I am more interested in building. So, I think that is what always gives me sanity; I mean, the joy of it and the passion behind that."

No matter how big the business grew or what the profits looked like, the urge to run it like a one-woman business perhaps never left. After all, it has been said that if you want to go fast, go alone. And she likes to go fast. "Starting the business is actually the easiest thing to do," she remarks. "It is maintaining it and growing it that is more complicated."

While she has grown to see the importance of structure, she has at times not had the patience to go through the process and has fallen back on old habits, corporate structure be damned. Still, she sees value in having people who can voice concerns objectively.

For all the success that the Manet Group has achieved, whether it is in establishing Manet Housing, Manet Paradise, Manet Construction, or Manet Towers, she will be the first to admit that she could not have done it on her own.

She advises up-and-coming entrepreneurs to surround themselves with people who are unafraid to speak their minds, even when their views may be contrary to those of the business owner or the lead executive.

While the visionary model may move the company out of the blocks, it will crumble if there is no real structure as it grows. And though she may not like the boxed-in feeling of structure, she has grudgingly accepted it as a crucial component for success.

Out of the ashes of failure, the Manet Group began. Since then, Tess has leaned on her faith in God, insisting that it is 200% of her entire success. She continues to encounter failures, but now, she's in too deep; she's having too much fun.

Theresa is living her dream.

CHAPTER 8

PULLING IT ALL TOGETHER

"Life is like a grinding stone, whether it polishes you up or grinds you down depends on the stuff you are made of."

Unknown

In the chapters above, we have witnessed the amazing stories, motivations, and obstacles our cohort of featured entrepreneurs have encountered, endured and beaten to attain the success level they have reached.

Throughout the stories certain skills, characteristics, and attitudes seem to be the driving forces that have propelled them despite the obstacles encountered. One thing that is clear is that obstacles were both extrinsic and intrinsic but through it all our featured entrepreneurs more than survived. They excelled. The big question is, what are the common traits that stick out as the principal springboards for their success?

This concluding chapter will attempt to map out some of these characteristics not as an attempt at a traits theory but as a guide for parents and future entrepreneurs to nurture these skills and characteristics in our bid to produce future persons who will take on the mantle of the next phase of growing businesses despite our seemingly hostile business and entrepreneurial environment. That is the only direction towards achieving self-sufficiency in our development agenda and providing jobs to the teeming youth.

Examiningthevariousstoriesbringsoutcertaincommonalities among all our featured entrepreneurs. These include, but are not limited to:

(a). Holding on to a long-term vision, picture, idea, or motivation, and irrespective of the blurredness or seeming unachievability of the dream, they still held on steadfastly to that hope. In some sense, one could describe it as obstinate optimism, crazy and rash decision making in the face of stable and secured situations.

(b). Our entrepreneurs chose to follow their instincts as in the case of Tony Oteng-Gyasi and Gwyneth Gyimah Addo, who found themselves in leaving promising, secured stable jobs on fast tracks with multinational companies. They chose to jump into the unknown and unstable world of starting their own businesses. They would not be dissuaded from pursuing this dream, no matter how many times they crashed holding on to this picture.

It is evident that some of these traits that we find recurring among our group did not suddenly emerge when they grew up, but traces of these were evident during their childhood and growing up phase of their lives. Examples of these are selling milk powder and organising parties as in the case of Gwyneth Gyimah Addo, trading baseball cards as Kofi Anku did, and selling condensed milk toffees like Leticia Osafo-Addo.

These were all little pet projects that were developing the inner entrepreneurial instincts of their young minds and nurturing them to fruition.

Another significant trait from the life of our entrepreneurs is the fact that most of them displayed what will be described as stubbornness in their childhood, which was actually a strong will to pursue whatever they set their hearts on. This attitude came in handy when the tough times in the development of their businesses came along. It is this trait that sustained them and kept them going. This is indicative that it is not all that negative for one to have a strong determined will, especially when noticed in children. It should be nurtured and channelled.

The general attitude among most parents is to cut that attitude to size through actions that break the confidence of the child. This is because they find it difficult to deal with an independent-minded child in a culture where blind obedience to the dictates of parents or older persons is regarded as the appropriate mode of behaviour. A proper nurturing of this trait will eventually inure to the benefit of the adult in their most trying times should they decide to embark on entrepreneurial ventures.

Innovation, which is a bedrock for successful enterprise growth and development, does not only mean new ideas but also new and better ways of executing projects and plans. All our cohort group members displayed varying degrees of innovation from products through delivery mechanisms to convenience systems, and these have been what has guaranteed the sustenance of their entrepreneurial exploits.

Therefore, another important characteristic and trait is the constant scouring of their operating environments to pick up signs and signals of new innovations that will be needed to keep the businesses relevant.

Strong intrinsic motivation to create solutions to issues around them in the social and business ecosystem seems to have been a major driving force for our cohort group rather than financial rewards. This is what has kept them moving on to a bigger scale rather than being content with what would have given them and their families financial comforts. Without this driving force, most of their enterprises would either have been short-lived or remained at subsistence levels. This is strongly linked to courage to enter the business environment and take the risk, especially in a hostile business environment as we have in Ghana.

Risk seems to be a predominant variable anytime entrepreneurship is mentioned. What is missing from the lexicon, however, is that it takes courage to even attempt to engage in anything that has the potential of being risky. This courage is displayed by our entrepreneurs in either throwing the chance of cushy jobs to the wind or risking the little capital at their disposal towards their ventures without regard to the consequence of the venture not yielding the desired results. Our cohort group has displayed the will and desire to pick themselves up when a venture fails. They however did not shy away from entering the arena of creating and investing in a new venture. Resilience and the courage to soldier on despite obstacles, therefore, is a strong trait of successful entrepreneurs and leaders.

Another interesting trait displayed by our group is the will to quickly forget disappointments, especially from people they trusted, and just plod on as if nothing happened. Our group chose to live on for tomorrow rather than brood about yesterday. Disappointments were treated as passing clouds or storms or expensive educational fees for the knowledge gained from the disappointments.

Strong ethical actions and behaviours seem to be common among our group. This goes contrary to the popular belief that private enterprises indulge in unethical practices to achieve the growth and development they achieve. Whilst not indicating that unethical practices do not exist within the private sector, our featured group was concerned about the display of unethical attitudes and behaviours from their staff or partners.

Another strong trait coming out of our group is a strong religious leaning or belief in spirituality. In spite of their skills and efforts to grow the businesses, they are not full of boast. Their general feeling is that their success is not just happenstance and that an invisible hand has been kind to them.

The commonalities of some of the characteristics among our cohort group lend credence to the fact that even though entrepreneurs can be made, certain traits must be present to augment the skills. What this implies is that not everyone can be an entrepreneur even if trained. There are points along the entrepreneurship journey when traits developed during childhood come in handy and that is what ensures the resilience and tenacity that is needed to weather the tough times.

The foregoing points also bring out issues that our society is very guilty of, and which sometimes shatters entrepreneurial instincts as children grow. This tends to create docility among many potential future entrepreneurs. The Ghanaian society looks down on hand-skilled professions for educated persons. We prefer liberal education that will create white-collar jobs. Even though the current educational system encourages some vocational trades this is treated contemptuously, with weaker students pushed in that direction. We see further evidence of their relegation with the accompanying derogation of those who opt for those programmes.

The narratives from our featured entrepreneurs indicate that the steely resolve to plod on, when everyone would have thought that they were seeing and chasing mirages rather than realities, presents the case that these characteristics and traits have been developed over a long period of time, specifically during their childhoods.

This brings up the question and issue of the parental role in nurturing or killing these instincts and traits as children grow up. The Ghanaian society has a peculiar attitude to independent minded and strong-willed children and all efforts are made to stamp out what is classified as stubbornness. This is further reinforced at the school level, especially the basic school level, where massive efforts are made to "straighten" these seemingly wayward behaviours.

However, as is obvious from our stories, this steely resolve is a clear precedent for successful entrepreneurship. Developing that tenacious spirit stands one in good stead when the tough times come during the early phases of business development. Parents need to identify and recognise these early signs as positive and direct them through a proper nurturing phase rather than demonise these behaviours, and they should be able to explain to the children's schools so that together with the teachers the formative years for these budding entrepreneurial prospects can be properly nurtured.

It is obvious from the stories that the beginnings are quite tough, and one needs to reach into one's inner strength to continue to plod on and to achieve the success that we are so eager to celebrate. There are no profits if there are no costs and so keeping eyes open to spot the traits early in the child's development will stand the family and the larger country in good stead in developing businesses that will create the employment avenues for our ever-growing youthful population.

Another issue our discussion throws up is the Ghanaian concept of a job. A relic of our colonial heritage is how we regard self-employment versus being employed by someone. Our concept of a job is when one is employed in an enterprise by someone. We, therefore, do not encourage entrepreneurial exploits, especially if the person has had tertiary education. The concept of a well-placed position is in a formal establishment of which start-ups are not considered as one. So, apart from attempts to snuff out entrepreneurial traits at the early formative years, those who survive that and attempt to start out something for themselves are discouraged and frowned upon, especially if the venture happens to require manual input e.g., farming, hairdressing, dressmaking, catering, etc.

These are considered ventures for people who could not withstand the rigours of formal education at the highest level. A change in attitude at the societal level will go a long way in encouraging our young people to see the job as what puts food on their table and not what is regarded as prestigious.

Finally, the major lifeblood for any enterprise development is financing. This is a critical requirement, because without it all good ideas stagnate at the ideation stage. All major economies that have become developed had their banking sectors as the major thrust. Unfortunately for us in Ghana, the reverse is true. No bank in Ghana is interested in funding a start-up but are quick to chase for the business once the enterprise has achieved growth status. This is what is stifling the growth of enterprises in Ghana. Most entrepreneurs in our cohort group have had to reach deep down into their pockets or have had to take Shylock loans to finance their enterprises.

Little wonder most of the enterprises have remained as small and medium enterprises (SME). Moving up to scale is unable to feature in the dictionaries of most entrepreneurs. It is thus commendable that our cohort group, having faced this harsh banking and financial terrain, has not only survived but thrived to provide a contribution to the easing of the unemployment burden.

Every year the banks declare large profits, mostly earned through investment in Government securities. It is the belief of the author that should all the banks agree to put 1% of their profits into start-ups or venture capital financing, the story in 10 years will be very different, with the economy buoyant and a lot more jobs being created to ease the unemployment burden of the country. The banks in Ghana are indulging in the proverbial "cutting one's nose to spite one's face".

A change in attitude by the banks can only be driven by policy changes offering incentives for those who would be willing to finance start-ups. Additionally, our universities should stop turning out book literates solely designed for pen-pushing which jobs are now very few and start introducing entrepreneurial modules as part of the compulsory courses students must study throughout the undergraduate programmes. By so doing, a corps of university students will be attracted and drift towards developing enterprises in singles or in groups. With the requisite financing from the banks as earlier intimated, this should provide the transformative boost to the creation of the next crop of business owners and leaders and help mitigate the unemployment situation.

A growing population with a huge unemployment burden requires innovative and creative thinking and the surest route is to create the desire as well as the enabling environment for young people to become interested in the creation of jobs, rather than looking up to the public and corporate sector that currently seems oversubscribed to solve this problem.

The stories of the six successful entrepreneurs told in this book should become not only an inspirational piece for the young, but also a springboard for officialdom to start dismantling the obstacles through policy initiatives that will ginger and encourage the Ghanaian youth to start looking at self-employment in the first instance and growth of their enterprises to be able to employ others.

EPILOGUE

"Everything started as nothing."

Ben Weissenstein, CEO and Founder, The Entitled Group

Enterprises are created to solve, deliver, or generate solutions to emerging issues through the offer of products or services. However, enterprise creation starts because there is nothing that sufficiently solves the issue at hand. In the process, time, energy, capital, ingenuity, and skills come into play to ensure the creation not only happens but lasts. The measure of any successful enterprise, therefore, is the ability to ensure continuity in the absence of the founder.

Ensuring a legacy is based on lessons and knowledge that can be transmitted from one generation to the next. Entrepreneurs should continue to articulate their life goals all along the way. Having a personal mission statement that is written and kept before their eyes is a sure way to ensure that deviations from the original mission that made the business can survive changes in leadership.

Our case study cohort group has braved the odds and established enterprises that are now regarded as mainstream, providing several jobs that probably would have been nonexistent. When all is said and done, creating jobs and opportunities for young persons to be able to be productive for the country is all that matters.

Government jobs are just a fraction of what job opportunities can be available in the country. Thus, the private sector has the onerous responsibility of shouldering this burden by being an effective and efficient engine to spur on the growth of employment opportunities. However, with such a harsh terrain for the growth of enterprises, it is hoped the field will be levelled through proactive policies to encourage the private sector to grow, otherwise mass unemployment is what will be the bane of this country.

Young persons should not only be encouraged to work for themselves but also to provide the policy environment for them to be able to start enterprises and to thrive. Additionally, a major behavioural change needs to be promoted among the populace for enterprise creation to become the sought-after vocation rather than the current practice where everyone is looking to get employed by a government office or a mainstream organisation.

We need to create a culture of people wanting to become employers rather than employees.

Once upon a time everything that exists now started as nothing. What made them happen were opportunities that were taken advantage of and despite the difficulties, we have businesses that have become successful because their owners chose the path of tenacity and resilience. Today, we can celebrate them, but we need more wins that will carry on with the mantle for succeeding generations.

A new cohort group of entrepreneurs needs to be nurtured and encouraged to move up to scale. The ball is in the court of the Ghanaian society to ensure that we can continually create jobs that will be able to absorb the teeming numbers of young people who come onto the job market every year.

The process of enacting various policy directives that will put emphasis on the opportunities for the private sector to become the lifeline for employment ought to start now. The stories shared in this book are also to motivate and encourage young people to take the plunge. The future of the country is through entrepreneurship, not public-sector jobs. The time to begin this emphasis is now.

REFERENCES

1. Jon L Pierce and Newstrom: Leaders and the Leadership process: Readings, Assessments, and Application. McGraw-Hill Higher Education 2nd Edition 2000

2. Phillip M Podsakoff, Scott Mackenzie, Robert Moorman, and Richard Fetter: Transformational Leader Behaviors and Their Effects on Followers' Trust in Leader, Satisfaction and Organizational Citizenship Behaviors. Reading 40. Jon L Pierce and Newstrom: Leaders and the Leadership Process: Readings, Assessments, and Application. McGraw-Hill Higher Education 2nd Edition, 2000

3. Timmons 1991 Model as cited by Richard Dellarbarca MBA Thesis (2002) University of Cambridge Judge School of Business

4. Richard J Goossen and R Paul Stevens: Entrepreneurial Leadership: Finding Your Calling, Making a Difference. InterVarsity Press IL. 2013

5. Scott Shane: A General Theory of Entrepreneurship: The Individual to Opportunity Nexus: Edward Elgar Publishing 2003

6. Interviews with Tony Oteng Gyasi, 2007, Theresa Oppong-Beeko, 2018, Leticia Osafo-Addo, 2019, Kofi Anku, 2019, Kwasi Appeagyei, 2020, Gwyneth Gyimah Addo, 2020.

Alex Banful is a seasoned marketing professional with over forty years of experience in Ghana and across Africa. His expertise spans several industries, including FMCG, Computers, Consulting, and Public Health, and functions, including behaviour change communication. He has a proven track record over three decades of social marketing design and implementing blockbuster social behavior change programmes within the health sector in Ghana, including the very successful national campaigns for HIV/Aids – "Stop Aids Love Life" and Family Planning – "It's your life, it's your choice". His work helped to curb the HIV menace in Ghana and made contraceptives for population management a part of normal society presence.

Alex has also mentored several business people and entrepreneurs over the years, and together with his combined experience leading GSMF International, has observed much about the social environment for entrepreneurship development in Ghana. As a firm proponent of entrepreneurship and the private sector as a sustainable engine for growth and employment, he has now turned his attention to changing the local environment and is committed to incept a change in the social narrative and perception of young, educated Ghanaians being motivated to both create enterprises that would create livelihoods for others and to also work for themselves. Indeed, this paradigm shift is important if we are to create avenues for employment for an ever-growing workforce.

Alex was born in 1955, studied at Accra Academy for his "O" and "A", level Certificates. He received a Bachelor of Arts in Political Science (1977) from the University of Ghana and an Executive Master's in Governance and Leadership from GIMPA Graduate School Greenhill (2003). He holds full membership of the Chartered Institute of Marketing Ghana

Printed in Great Britain
by Amazon

78686312R00112